YOUR VOICE
at CITY HALL

SUNY Series in Urban Public Policy
Mark Schneider and Richard Rich, Editors

YOUR VOICE
at CITY HALL

THE POLITICS, PROCEDURES
AND POLICIES OF
DISTRICT REPRESENTATION

Peggy Heilig *and*
Robert J. Mundt

STATE UNIVERSITY OF NEW YORK PRESS
Albany

Published by
State University of New York Press, Albany

© 1984 State University of New York

Printed in the United States of America

For information, address State University of New York Press, State University Plaza, Albany, N.Y., 12246

Library of Congress Cataloging in Publication Data

Heilig, Peggy, 1942-
    Your voice at city hall.

    (SUNY series in urban public policy)
    Includes bibliographical references.
    1. Local elections—United States. 2. Elect
districts—United States. 3. City councilmen—United
States. 4. Municipal government—United States.
I. Mundt, Robert J. II. Title. III. Series: SUNY series
on urban public policy.
JS395.H44 1984   324.6′3   83-24287
ISBN 0-87395-821-7
ISBN 0-87395-820-9 (pbk.)

10 9 8 7 6 5 4 3 2 1

Contents

Acknowledgment

I want to thank whatever Fates sent me to UNC-Charlotte where Bob Mundt and I began the collaboration that produced this manuscript. Mere thanks cannot express my appreciation for his support and his willingness to put up with my many extra-professional judgments. My friends Jane Miles, Barbara Leone, Judy Jones, Kathy Kutsche, and Molly Waite listened to much more about this project than they ever wanted to hear. The officials I met in Des Moines and Peoria were knowledgeable, interesting and gracious; they and their counterparts in other cities are the true urban experts. Most of all, I want to thank the champion of Hoops for keeping my mind on truly important things.

PH
Urbania, Illinois
June 22, 1984

The reader must indulge us in some mutual admiration. The germ of this project came from Peggy Heilig's observation of the Charlotte fight over districts in 1977. As a good political scientist, she saw the potential in that experience for a general study of district representation, and contributed the initiative, the insight, and the drive without which it would not have been accomplished. Among our collaborators on the project, special credit goes to Arnold Fleischmann for work "above and beyond the call of duty" in data-gathering and analysis in the Texas cities, for drafting the description of Ft. Worth, and in helpful reflection on the entire study. David Cox provided the information base from Memphis and Montgomery, and Aida Riddell from sacramento. Charles Cotrell assisted in this effort for Dallas and San Antonio. Jamie Garriss, Alex Pearce, Michelle Hill, Mary Lou Foy, Lee Ann Brown, and Alberto Gonzalez participated in data collection. Anna Howie prepared the index. The Center for the Study of Metropolitan Problems, National Institute of Mental Health, provided the financial support for our research under Project No. 5R01MH33128-02, ably administered by Dick Wakefield. Mary McGinnis transformed our very rough drafts into impeccable copy. My wife Carol demonstrated patience and good cheer during long hours committed to a project that was not high on her list of personal priorities; may she somehow be rewarded for it someday.

RJM
Charlotte, North Carolina
June 28, 1984

1

Urban Reform and Its Contemporary Consequences

WHAT DIFFERENCE does it make if city council members are elected at large, or by geographically defined districts or wards? It made a difference to the urban reformers of the Progressive Movement: They saw at-large elections as a potent weapon in their battle against political machines. Nearly a century later, it makes a difference to leaders of minority groups: They have gone to court to challenge the constitutionality of at-large systems, and they have organized petition drives and referenda campaigns aimed at replacing at-large with district elections.

During the 1970s, district systems were adopted in one-third of the southern cities with substantial black populations that were electing councils at-large at the beginning of that decade. Have political, procedural, and policy changes resulted from those shifts to district councils?

Like most rules, electoral procedures are not neutral. At-large systems favor the electoral chances of certain groups of urban dwellers; theoretically, at least, district elections should favor other groups, and changes from at-large to district systems should lead to new patterns of power and benefit distribution. The question we will attempt to answer here is whether recent structural shifts to district elections have, in fact, had consequences for local politics, procedures and policy.

THE ORIGINS OF AT-LARGE REPRESENTATION

When the urban wing of the Progressive Movement fought political machines for control of American cities, these reformers wanted not only to "throw the rascals out"; they also wanted to make certain that local offices would be denied in the future to persons connected with boss-led, ethnically based machines. To the reform-minded citizens engaged in that conflict, at-large elections of city council members were both a means to an end and an end in themselves.

Instrumentally, at-large electoral systems were one of the means used to destroy the effectiveness of the urban machines which emerged in most large cities during the mid- and late nineteenth century. Such organizations, put together by politically skilled entrepreneurs from immigrant—usually Irish—backgrounds, were a byproduct of the Industrial Revolution in the United States. (Judd, 1979: 26–42). In response to industrial development, millions of foreigners migrated to this country to work in manufacturing, mining and construction. Poor, uneducated, unskilled, often Catholic in a Protestant land, and speaking only their native languages, immigrants clustered in their adopted cities by country of origin. Since the governments of industrializing cities generally included councils elected by districts (called, then, as in many areas today, wards), effective political organizations could be built on the dual foundations of geographically bound electoral districts and the residential clustering of European ethnics. As Judd explains:

> The decentralized nature of local politics facilitated ethnic political power. The basic electoral unit, the precinct, rarely included more than 600 to 800 voters. Aldermen sitting on city councils typically represented wards containing forty or fifty precincts. Patterns of ethnic segregation guaranteed that some wards would be dominated by lower-class Irish, others by Italians, and still other by native Protestants.
>
> The decentralized structure of the urban political system, combined with mass suffrage and ethnic residential segregation, led to a style of politics in which social and political relationships became highly interconnected. Political success could be gained through social prominence. Thus, most large American cities went through "friends and neighbors" or "local followings" style of politics in which local leaders—very often pub owners—came to dominate first a precinct and then a ward. Mature party machines simply linked these local leaders together in mutually supportive alliances.
>
> (1979: 55)

Because machine politics was ethnic-based, urban reform was not, of course, either ethnically or socially neutral. Conflict between machines and reformers is correctly viewed as a conflict between cultures. Harrigan describes it this way:

> The machine leaders rose from the working and lower classes in the immigrant communities. In contrast, the reformers were primarily upper-class and upper-middle-class business people, lawyers, professionals and university people. There were some sharp ideological differences within the ranks of the reformist movement, but, in contrast to the machine politicians, the reformers shared many traits. Rather than being immigrants or first-generation Americans, the reformers came from families that had lived in America for generations. They were Protestant rather than Catholic, and very often they had graduated from colleges and professional schools rather than being poorly educated. Rather than conducting their occupational affairs through personal and old fashioned informal methods as did the political machine leaders, the reformers came from occupations in which they had mastered modern, rational and quasi-scientific methods of organization. Individually, they came from an antiurban heritage that placed considerable value on individual initiative, agricultural life, and a town meeting form of democracy. Somewhat at odds with their belief in democracy was their elitist belief that government should be conducted by the best-educated and best-qualified people in the society.
>
> (1981: 89)

Where the progressives were successful in establishing at-large council elections, it became difficult for the nonaffluent to gain council seats. Candidates could no longer depend upon election with only the support of their own ethnic group or of a small section of their community; city-wide campaigns required more time, more money, and more social standing than working class status could provide.

At-large elections were an important feature of both the original Progressive reform plan, the commission system, and its successor, the council-manager plan. As an end in itself, the new electoral mechanism, along with nonpartisanship, was expected to result in the election of a "better" class of citizen to local councils. Following the establishment of the first commission government in Galveston and shortly thereafter in several other Texas cities and in Des Moines, Iowa, businessmen in many other cities worked to replace mayor-ward council governments with commissions. According to Schiesl

Behind these developments lay the more important effort to place more wealthy businessmen in office. In line with their counterparts in large cities, many politically oriented capitalists in smaller communities were young representatives of advanced segments of relatively new industries which had come to dominate urban economic life. They felt that public policy should be consistent with the inherent rationalization in corporate systems and sought to bring order to metropolitan life. Toward this end they sought to reduce the influence of lower- and middle-income groups in public decision making. Before the adoption of the commission system, the typical ward-elected alderman was a small businessman, skilled artisan or unskilled worker. But now upper-class businessmen were determined to change the social backgrounds of city officials.

(1977: 139)

The ultimate goal of the reformers was, thus, control by one socioeconomic group, not equal representation of all elements of a local polity. As Schiesl states,

the goal of the commission movement was far from democratic in the traditional sense of proposing more popular control over public policy. In the minds of business leaders, the issue was not to make representative decisions. Rather, it was a question of having the right people in government to make the correct decisions.

(1977: 139–140)

Sometimes implicitly, but usually explicitly, municipal reformers assumed that such a monopoly of power would lead to more efficient government which would be beneficial for the entire community. Political conflict was to be replaced by an apolitical business model in which policy formulation would be separate from administration; decision making would be rational and scientific,[1] free of influence from partisan or "selfish" interests. That vision of a properly run city became a blueprint for "good government" with the publication of the Municipal League's influential Model City Charter of 1915, in which the League recommended adoption of the council-manager form of government, civil service employment, and at-large, nonpartisan elections. Of these structures and procedures, only at-large elections have become the subject of controversy in contemporary urban settings.

THE LEGACY OF AT-LARGE REPRESENTATION

In some large, industrialized cities such as Chicago, St. Louis, and Cleveland, reformers never succeeded in eliminating ward elections. However, the inclusion of at-large elections in the original Model City Charter and its various revisions led to the adoption of this form of election in thousands of new or growing cities during the first half of the twentieth century. This was particularly true of cities in the South and the West, regions which urbanized in the twentieth rather than the nineteenth century; in the mid-seventies, 74 percent of southern cities and 79 percent of western cities elected councils at large, compared to 51.6 percent of eastern and 50.2 percent of midwestern cities (Sanders, 1979).

While European ethnics were the original groups disadvantaged by at-large elections, a substantial body of evidence supports the claim that blacks are the group currently disadvantaged by the system. Urban reformers of the early twentieth century were not, of course, concerned about possible election of blacks to city councils; their preferred procedure, however, is inherently biased against any geographically concentrated minority which cannot gain substantial voting support from the majority group. As southern blacks became more urbanized and more politically assertive, the contemporary effects of at-large representation became apparent.

Scholarly attention to the possible bias of at-large representation began in the early 1960s when several influential scholars argued that the financial costs, organizational demands, and need for widespread name recognition associated with city-wide campaigns made it difficult for persons removed from leadership circles to conduct successful campaigns. Negative attitudes towards minority groups were identified as an additional factor making it difficult for minority candidates to win at-large elections. (Banfield and Wilson, 1963, 89–96; Hays, 1964). This analysis of local governmental structure signaled a break from earlier academic support for progressive reforms. As Lineberry (1978) reminds us, the early political science profession was in the vanguard of that effort.

More recently, the theoretical linkages between urban structure and possible underrepresentation of minorities suggested by Banfield/Wilson and Hays have been tested empirically by political scientists using a variety of data bases and several different measures of representational equity. These studies have focused on the question of whether at-large systems are biased against blacks.

As reviewed by Robinson and Dye (1978), the first empirical studies did not utilize nationwide data. Sloan (1969) studied the twenty-eight largest American cities, concluding that the proportion of council seats held by blacks was closest to black population proportions under district systems of election. Campbell and Feagin (1975) looked at council membership in forty-six southern cities with populations over 100,000. Thirty-seven of these cities had at-large elections: Blacks had gained membership on just eighteen, or 48.6 percent, of these legislatures. On the other hand, blacks were members of seven of eight mixed councils, that is, councils with some seats elected at large and others elected by district.

Karnig (1976) produced the first cross-sectional study of the impact of political structure on minority representation. Using data from 139 cities with populations over 25,000 and which were at least 15 percent black, he found that district systems do facilitate election of blacks to city councils, especially in the North. Karnig was also the first to devise a scale for measuring the equity of minority representation; his representational equity scores were created by dividing percentage of blacks on council by percentage of blacks in a city's population.

Karnig's conclusions have been supported in a number of other studies. Robinson and Dye (1978) utilized data from all SMSA central cities which are at least 15 percent black and found that at-large elections significantly reduced black representation independently of any other structural arrangements or any socioeconomic factors. Latimer's (1979) analysis of data from eighty cities in Alabama, Louisiana and South Carolina echoed those results. Taebel (1978) reached similar conclusions with still another data set—those SMSA central cities where blacks would have a statistical chance of gaining a council seat in a district system—and with a different measure of equity, calculated by subtracting black population percentages from black council proportions. Taebel also found that council size was significantly related to black equity, but that controlling for size did not affect the link between districts and increased equity.

Karnig and Welch (1980) looked at electoral systems as one of a wide range of demographic and structural factors which potentially may influence black candidacy rates and black membership on councils. Using data from all cities over 25,000 in population and at least 10 percent black, they find that district elections are positively associated with both candidate and representational equity. Although concluding that the most important factor associated with the election of blacks to city councils is black resources, they state that:

This information tends to reinforce the arguments of activists who have brought court challenges against the use of at-large elections, claiming that they discriminate against blacks. The provision of district elections is evidently the most important variable that can be politically manipulated to improve the opportunity for equitable black representation on city councils.

(1980: 99)

Using the same data set as Robinson and Dye, Engstrom and McDonald (1981) have challenged the conclusion that black resources have a greater impact on representational equity than does electoral structure. Introducing a more sophisticated measure of representation, one that treats proportionality between black population and black council membership as a relationship across cities rather than as a dependent variable, they used regression techniques to determine the effect on black representational equity of proportion black of the population under various conditions of electoral structure and demographics. Their findings show that while the differential between black and community income had the greatest impact on black representation where blacks make up only a small percentage of the population, once the proportion black reaches 15 percent, electoral structure becomes the most important determinant of representational equity; once again, district elections are linked to higher levels of black equity.

Only two studies, those by Cole (1974) and MacManus (1978) fail to find a relationship between electoral structure and black representation. Cole's study was based on only a small number of cases, sixteen New Jersey cities; MacManus, who divided elections into seven categories (At-Large, No Residency Restrictions; At-Large, with Seat or Position Restrictions; At-Large, with District Residency Requirements for All Seats; At-Large, Combination of District Residency and Positional Seats; Partially Mixed; Mixed; Single-Member Districts) found blacks underrepresented by all electoral plans.

Clearly considerable attention has been given to the alleged underrepresentation of blacks in at-large systems; however, little attention has yet been given to the question of whether electoral structure affects representational equity for the nation's newest and fastest-growing minority, persons of Spanish origin. Only Taebel (1978) and MacManus (1978) have looked at this relationship. Taebel found that while more equitable representation for Hispanics appears linked to district elections, the relationship disappears when council size is taken into account. He suggests that the difference in the way electoral structure affects blacks and Hispanics may be due to less residential concentration of Hispanics, concluding that Hispanics might be better served by attempting to enlarge councils rather than working for adoption of district elections. On the other hand, MacManus found that Hispanics as well as blacks were disadvantaged by each of her seven electoral types.

Regardless of this minor disagreement among academics as to the actual impact of different electoral arrangements, referenda campaigns and court actions aimed at replacing at-large with district systems occurred so frequently in the 1970s that in the Sunbelt states, at least, these efforts are one of the dominant trends in local politics during that decade. In the minds of many local minority leaders, the effect of at-large elections was clear: At-large elections were making it difficult, sometimes impossible, for them to win council seats.

LOCAL REPRESENTATION AND CIVIL RIGHTS

An obvious ancestor to the movement toward districts is the Civil Rights Movement of the 1960s; district advocacy shares that movement's concern with citizen equity. More specifically, the question in the challenge to at-large elections is "whether or not one person because of his race is prevented from affecting the electoral process leading to nominations and election more than some other person." (Claunch and Hallman, 1978:1)

The origins of the district movement as a civil rights weapon are in two strands of activity at the federal level. In judicial proceedings, the Supreme Court's rulings on apportionment beginning with *Baker v. Carr* (396 U.S. 186, 1962) were used by minorities to keep the courts in the political thicket concerning equal voting rights. *Baker v. Carr* concerned place of residence rather than race, but the Court's attention was turned to the racial issue by the second area of activity: Congressional actions of 1963, 1964, and 1965, which changed the political rules of the game in the South. The Voting Rights Act of 1965 received the most attention immediately after passage for its provision of federal voting registrars and the consequent dramatic rise in the number of black registered voters. In spite of the cautions advanced by reliable observers (see Matthews' and Prothro's conclusion, 1966: 477–481), there were great expectations that obtaining the franchise would translate into black office holders and new directions in public policy. A certain amount of frustration was inevitable when few blacks were elected to top level offices, except by black-majority electorates.

Section Five of the 1965 Voting Rights Act received less attention initially. That section required state and local governments to submit for preclearance any proposed change in voting practices or procedures to the Justice Department or the U.S. District Court for the District of Columbia. Leaders in the Civil Rights movement were aware of a historical pattern in which efforts to legislate voting rights had been frustrated by ingenious technical barriers; Section Five was meant to strip southern lawmakers of such opportunity.

Even before the 1965 legislation, southerners had the at-large election procedure in their defensive arsenal. For example, in 1962 the Mississippi legislature adopted a number of measures, including at-large elections, to restrict black voting; these actions were in response to concerns that the movement of blacks into cities might produce all-black wards. The sponsor of a proposal to elect city councils at-large stated that the legislation was needed in order "to maintain our southern way of life." Contemporary news accounts were unambiguous about their purpose: The headline in the *Jackson Daily News* of February 23, 1962 was "Bill Would Make it Harder for Negroes to Win Election." (U.S. Commission on Civil Rights, 1975: 284). After passage of the Voting Rights Act, the Mississippi legislature moved to change the vote for county supervisors from district to at-large, and chose not to submit the change to Justice or the federal court. Two years later, Joseph Rauh could conclude that

> precisely because Negro registration has been successful, new roadblocks to political participation throughout the South have been thrown up at every available point. The Negro vote has been diluted by switching to at-large elections and by redrawing district lines, thus diminishing the influence that would otherwise be drawn from concentrations of Negro voting strength.
>
> (Rauh, 1968: 9–10)

In 1969 the Supreme Court in *Allen v. State Board of Elections* (393 U.S. 544) ruled against the Mississippi statute and declared that it constituted a "voting qualification or prerequisite to voting, or standard, practice, or procedure with respect to voting," and was within the purview of the Section 5 requirement. Attention to the district/at-large question had been imposed on the civil rights movement's agenda, and would remain there throughout the 1970s.

THE MOVEMENT TO DISTRICTS

Two patterns, one regional and the other ethnic, describe the movement toward district councils. First, efforts to replace at-large elections occurred more frequently in the South than in other areas and, second, efforts were more frequent in cities where blacks rather than Hispanics are the largest minority group.

In order to assess the national scope of the district movement, we gathered data through mail surveys of city clerks and newspaper editors in the 385 American cities with populations over 10,000 which were at least 15 percent black in 1970 and the 156 cities over 10,000 which were at least 15 percent Hispanic.[2]

Looking first at the cities with substantial black populations, we find that in 1970, 83.5 percent of the southern and 54 percent of the northern cities elected councils at-large. During the 1970s, one-third of the southern cities changed to district or mixed systems, while another 22 percent either experienced unsuccessful attempts or were in the midst of pro-district efforts in early 1981. Outside the South, 16.1 percent of the at-large cities adopted districts and 5.4 percent witnessed attempts that failed. In 1970, in our subset of American cities, 75 percent of the at-large cities were located in the South; during the seventies, 87 percent of the changes to district and 93 percent of the unsuccessful attempts took place in that region.[3]

Turning to cities with at least 15 percent Hispanic population, over 92 percent elected councils at-large in 1970; during the next ten years, 8.4 percent adopted districts and another 7.6 percent experienced unsuccessful campaigns. As Table 1.1 indicates, movements to districts were more likely in cities where blacks are the major minority group, especially in the South.[4]

What factors motivated or influenced efforts to replace at-large with district systems? In southern cities, there is a strong link between the equity level of past black council membership and the district movement. Beginning with Karnig's (1976) measure of representational equity (created by dividing the percentage of blacks on council by the percentage of blacks in the population), we created an average equity value for the 1970s, or for the years in that decade before a change to districts. Attempts to establish districts were found in 59 percent of the southern cities in which blacks had never, in modern times, been elected to council; such actions were found in 36 perent of the cities with low to moderate equity levels, and in only 16 percent of the cities with relatively high equity scores.[5]

Table 1.1. At-large Cities in 1970 with Prodistrict Efforts in 1970s.

Cities Over 10,000 Which Are:	Adopted Districts	Unsuccessful Efforts
At least 15% black, in the South	33.1 (58)	22.0 (39)
At least 15% black, outside the South	16.1 (9)	5.4 (3)
At least 15% Hispanic	8.4 (10)	7.6 (9)

This relationship is not found in either the northern cities which are 15 percent black nor the cities which have substantial Hispanic populations. Relatively fewer northern cities had councils with no history of black membership; equity levels do vary in the North, but are not a motivating factor for district efforts there. Although one-third of the Hispanic cities (i.e., those which are at least 15 percent Hispanic) had no past representation by members of that group, only 7.5 percent of those cities reported district efforts; in comparison, 21 percent of the cities with low to moderate equity scores and 4.2 percent of those with relatively high equity levels saw attempts to establish districts, perhaps pointing to a curvilinear relationship in these locations.

The effect of percent minority also appears to differ among the three groups of cities. There is no relationship between these proportions and district efforts in northern or Hispanic cities, but in the South, efforts were more likely where blacks comprised at least 30 percent of the population. However, when past representational equity is taken into account, that relationship disappears, indicating again the overriding importance in the South of past black equity.

Finally, city size is a stronger explanatory factor for district movements in northern and Hispanic cities than it is in the South. Although 75 percent of the cities with substantial Hispanic populations have populations under 50,000, 63 percent (12) of the district efforts were found in cities over 50,000; over 36 percent of the larger cities experienced such actions. (See Table 1.2) In the North, where cities with substantial proportions of blacks are evenly divided between populations below and populations above 50,000, 79 percent of the district attempts occurred in the larger cities; 27 percent of those cities had pro-district activities. In the South, on the other hand, 42 percent of the smaller cities experienced district efforts, compared to 57 percent of the larger cities; however, in cities without any past black membership on council, efforts

Table 1.2. Percentage of Small and Large Cities with District Efforts.

Type of City	Under 50,000	Over 50,000
15% black, South	42.0	57.0
15% black, North	7.4	27.3
15% Hispanic	7.4	36.4

were found in 83 percent of the larger compared to 54 percent of the smaller cities. The view that larger cities provide a more open and pluralistic political arena and that minority groups tend to be better organized in big cities (Karnig and Welch, 1980: 19) is supported by these patterns. Further, minority leadership in larger cities may have more experience in political and legal activities, as well as more potential white allies than their counterparts in smaller cities.

Still, the district movement was found throughout the urban South, with efforts occurring in over 40 percent of the small cities which are at least 15 percent black. Matthews and Prothro (1966) found that the level of black participation was only slightly related to urbanization, and the scope of the southern district movement echoes those findings.

Current opposition to at-large elections, predominantly a southern phenomenon, and usually linked to demands and efforts of a black minority, does not have its roots in Progressive reform. The urban reformers wished to change the overall structure of local government to achieve two goals: Control by socioeconomic and technical elites which would, in turn, result in city governments being operated according to the precepts of scientific management. Contemporary district advocates, on the other hand, are concerned with representation rather than with the entire structure of local government, and with equality rather than control. In many of the cities where district efforts were mounted, blacks have little chance of winning a majority of council seats; district representation can be viewed as a means to the end of increased black representation but not as a catalyst of changes in other facets of local government. Implicit, however, in the behavior of district advocates is a faith in the pluralist notion that formal representation assures some influence in the decision-making process, or more simply and more symbolically, a belief that representational equity is an end in itself.

THE IMPACT OF DISTRICT REPRESENTATION

Prior research leads us to expect black representational equity to increase when cities begin electing at least some council seats by district. Assuming that outcome, what further expectations should we have, that is, what might be the consequences of increased proportions of minority members on city councils? Are there any relevant theoretical models upon which to base empirical predictions?

We turn, therefore, to consideration of two questions: "What *should* happen?" and "What *did* happen?" following actual changes to district elections. The *should* question will guide development of specific hypotheses concerning the impact of district representation. To determine the empirical validity of our hypotheses, the *did* questions will be answered with information obtained during two years of intensive observations in ten cities which recently adopted districts.

The overarching question motivating this inquiry is whether changes in electoral structure have multiple effects upon urban governance: Specifically, we are asking whether changes to districts will influence local politics, the procedures of council decision making, and the outcomes of such decisions. We did not—nor could we, of course—design this study to encompass all unanswered questions concerning urban representation, participation, decision-making or policy outcomes. By asking if districts make a difference, we do hope to address some unanswered questions in each of these areas.

NOTES

1   The reformers based many of their views concerning the proper way of running a city on the efficiency principles introduced by Frederick Winslow Taylor in *The Principles of Scientific Management*.

2   These data were obtained through two mail surveys, one of southern cities conducted in the summer of 1980 and a second of northern cities conducted in the summer of 1981. In an earlier (1978) survey of cities over 100,000, we found political editors of newspapers an excellent source of information concerning attempts to establish districts. Thus, in the southern survey, we began with a respondent group made up of political editors, following up with mailings to city clerks in nonresponding cities. Since the clerks' response rate was far superior—nearly 80 percent responded—clerks were the primary target group in the northern survey; while questionnaires were sent to editors in nonresponding cities, information on over 90 percent of our northern cases comes from clerks. We assume that editors outside major cities have too many roles to play to take the time for responding to mail questionnaires.

By categories we will be discussing, responses were received from 209 southern cities, 104 northern cities and 128 cities which are at least 15 percent Hispanic; the response rates are 82.3, 79.4 and 82.1 percent respectively.

The northern survey was conducted under a University of Illinois Graduate Research Board award; we wish to thank Michael LeRoy for assisting with data collection.

3 The southern states are Alabama, Arkansas, Georgia, Florida, Louisiana, Mississippi, North Carolina, South Carolina, Tennessee, Texas and Virginia. Northern States include California, Connecticut, Delaware, Illinois, Indiana, Kansas, Kentucky, Maryland, Massachusetts, Michigan, Missouri, Nevada, New Jersey, New York, Ohio, Oklahoma, Pennsylvania, West Virginia and Wisconsin.

There is no evidence that any movement to districts occurred before 1970 in the North. For example, during the 1960s four of our responding cities adopted districts and two efforts were unsuccessful.

4 Of the 19 pro-district efforts in cities which are at least 15 percent Hispanic, 9 occurred in Texas and 5 in California. These represent 27.5 percent of the relevant Texas cities, but only 7.4 percent of similar California cities.

5 In this measure of representational equity, a value of I indicates equity, values from 0.01 to 0.99 indicate decreasing levels of underrepresentation and values greater than I indicate overrepresentation. We use scores between 0.01 to 0.75 to show low to moderate levels of equity and scores higher than 0.75 to indicate relatively high equity levels. We begin the "relatively high" category with 0.76 because only eleven cases in the southern city group have scores above I.

2

Will Districts
Make a Difference?

O<small>NCE DISTRICTS</small> have been adopted, what other changes will follow? Many areas of local political life, including elections, interactions between council members and their constituents, council proceedings, and policy outcomes may be changed—slightly, moderately or radically—by the creation of districts. While there is no comprehensive theoretical framework from which to deduce specific predictions concerning the consequences of this modification of local electoral structure, selected theoretical assumptions and prior empirical findings from other approaches to urban governance may be helpful. In addition, logical extensions of what district advocates assume will occur once districts are in place can be utilized in the construction of hypotheses.

We will look at four specific aspects of urban political life—the politics of district elections, the process of representation, formal council proceedings and policy outcomes—in assessing the overall impact of district representation.

THE POLITICS OF DISTRICT ELECTIONS

Banfield and Wilson's (1963) early theorizing concerning the bias of at-large systems, along with substantial evidence that district elections are advantageous to black candidates, point directly to the expectation that more blacks will be elected to district councils whenever geographically concentrated blacks comprise a majority in one or more districts. Increases in Hispanic membership on city councils will also depend upon the residential clustering of that minority group. Naturally, the movement to districts will also result in councils with members residing throughout a city, not concentrated in more affluent areas.

Less simplistically, Banfield and Wilson (1963) also suggested that campaign requirements of the at-large process, particularly the expense of city-wide campaigns, discourage candidacies for council seats among the less affluent. If, indeed, facing a city-wide electorate discourages ambitious persons of white and blue collar status—regardless of race—from seeking office, the prospect of less expensive and less time-consuming district campaigns may encourage them to enter such races.

Districts might also result in the election of lower-status candidates. Although less-affluent voters rarely elect one of their own to executive or higher level legislative office, it is more likely that district voters might send a social equal to City Hall. Preference for "descriptive" representation (Pitkin, 1969: 10)—that is, representatives mirroring a constituency's demographic or cultural characteristics—is no longer very relevant to legislative bodies such as Congress, which have increasingly heterogeneous constituencies; however, such preferences might be important in the selection of local representatives. If so, a predominantly black district would not only elect a black to the council, but if a majority of the voters were of relatively low status they would prefer a clerk or a bus driver to a lawyer or a school administrator.

Turning to participation in local elections, findings from the most complete study of local voting (Alford and Lee, 1968) support the proposition that "reform" institutions, including at-large elections, are associated with lower voting rates. At the micro level, most studies have shown that high status persons cast votes in local elections more frequently than those of lower status (Lineberry and Sharkansky, 1979: 92–93). If these micro findings should hold across electoral structure, it is logical to expect increases in turnout among all socioeconomic groups with the advent of districts and if, as district advocates suggest, that form of election is strongly preferred in minority communities, the greatest increase in turnout should be seen in minority areas.

Sensible expectations of increased turnout, however must also include an assumption concerning competition; few observers or advocates would, or at least should, expect voters to turn out in large numbers for district elections that did not feature two serious, competitive candidates. On the other hand, it is not illogical to expect that the smaller scale of district elections will lead to hotly contested campaigns, especially in districts which are racially or ethnically heterogeneous.

Specifically, then, we will test the following hypotheses concerning local elections.

Once districts are established:

1. Racial and residential diversity among candidates and council members will increase.
2. More persons of white collar and blue collar status will run for council seats.
3. More persons of white collar and blue collar status will win council seats.
4. Campaign expenditures for council seats will decrease.
5. In competitive elections, voter turnout will increase over levels found for at-large elections.

THE PROCESS OF REPRESENTATION

Local representatives represent their constituents in a number of ways. They respond to, and sometimes encourage, individual or group requests and demands for services, facilities, or improvements in the performance of specific governmental tasks. In other words, they interact with constituents about questions or problems which do not necessarily concern an entire city. They also have a more general policy-making responsibility, that of participation in formal council actions which distribute public benefits and costs throughout a local populace; in this phase of representation, they may or may not be guided by the views of constituents. Both of these representation activities should be affected by changing from at-large to district systems of election.

We will begin by considering the orientation of local council members toward their constituents. Since the seminal conceptual work by Wahlke, Eulau, et al. (1959), these orientations, or styles of representation, have been discussed in terms of the delegate and trustee models.[1] Delegates make decisions in line with constituent wishes, while trustees decide on the basis of their own judgment. Several important congressional studies (Mayhew, 1974; Fiorina, 1977; Fenno, 1978) suggest the necessity of adding a third model of the representational role—that of ombudsman—if we are to properly categorize orientations of contemporary legislators.

Regardless of legislative arena, the ombudsman concept implies an emphasis upon serving individual members of a constituency in largely personal, noncontroversial ways. The traditional usage of the trustee concept to signify a reliance on one's own judgment and a concern for an entire polity is also as applicable in local settings as it is in state or national assemblies. However, while at the national level the concept of delegate usually indicates voting in accord with perceived wishes of a constituency, this category must be broadened at the local level to include a concern that geographic constituencies receive a sufficient share of public goods and services.

We believe that these models of role orientation will be applicable to local council members and, further, we expect district representatives to differ from at-large members in their representational style. Since district representatives have fewer constituents, they will not only be known by many district residents, but they will also have the opportunity to hear and see what matters concern "their people". Because city governments provide a wide variety of service on a day-to-day basis, and because individuals have problems with these services—the garbage is not picked up, the snow plow never arrives, the pothole needs filling, the stray dog won't leave the neighborhood—it would be surprising if district representatives did not adopt and practice the role of ombudsman.

Thus, we hypothesize the following role behavior for district council members, compared with at-large members of mixed councils or with members who served on at-large councils prior to the adoption of districts:

1. District representatives identify themselves as ombudsmen or delegates while at-large members see themselves as trustees.
2. District members have more citizen-initiated contacts with constituents than do at-large members.

A further concern is whether district representation affects interactions between council members—as individuals as well as collectively—and the administrative branch of city government. If district members take responsibility for the problems and needs of individual constituents do such actions result in unwanted intervention in bureaucratic operating procedures? This is our prediction:

3. District representatives assume a more activist role in processing citizen complaints than do at-large representatives.
4. Administrators will perceive district representatives as more likely to interfere with administrative procedures.
5. District representatives will stress willingness to follow council direction as a desirable administrative trait; at-large members are more likely to favor a strong leadership role for the city manager.

COUNCIL PROCEEDINGS: SETTING AGENDAS AND MAKING DECISIONS

Prevailing images of at-large councils picture those legislatures as groups of individuals recruited from the local "establishment" or "old boys' network" who deal with a limited number of issues, settle what disputes they have in private and, thus, rarely disagree in public. Such limiting of public decision making through control of the council agenda would fit the theoretical assumptions of Schattschneider's (1960: 30, 71) concept of mobilization of bias, in which values favoring dominant groups are built into institutional procedures, as well as Bachrach and Baratz's notion of non-decision-making. If there is issue limitation in at-large systems—if, as Bachrach and Baratz state in describing non-decision-making (1962: 948), "power . . . is exercised by confining the scope of decision-making to relatively 'safe' issues"—the explanation could be either that at-large elections can produce only councils which support dominant community or majority-group values, or that they produce councils whose members are effectively controlled by members of a "ruling elite". If either scenario correctly describes agenda setting by at-large councils, efforts to replace them with district legislatures can be viewed as reactions to what Cobb and Elder (1972) call systems of limited participation. It would follow logically that when such efforts succeed, they should have considerable impact upon council agendas and proceedings. Not only would the characteristics of individual council members become more heterogeneous, but at least some of the new representatives would raise those "dangerous" issues which had previously been denied a place on the council's agenda. We hypothesize, therefore that the adoption of districts will result in more public conflict among council members.

Specifically, we predict that conflict will arise over issues of redistribution and social services, public safety services, zoning and planning, and the decision-making process itself. Representatives of minority and lower-income neighborhoods will place higher priority on the importance and desirability of redistributive programs, and will have different perceptions of equity in the distribution and application of police and other protective services. We also expect that representatives of middle-class neighborhoods in cities still experiencing growth and expansion will oppose initiatives from supporters of contractors and developers in the areas of planning and zoning. Finally, we expect district representatives to disagree with at-large representatives, council members tied to the "old order," and members of the city bureaucracy over administrative issues such as the specifics of personnel and budgetary decisions, as district members attempt to gain influence over such matters by making them topics of open debate.

Because of the heterogeneity of interests, groups and areas represented on district councils, conflict during council proceedings will increase following the adoption of districts. Further, the increased conflict will be structured along the lines of competing interests within specific cities, but identifiable voting coalitions based on race, ethnicity or district demographics should emerge in each of our district councils.

We have already suggested that district representatives will see their role as that of an ombudsman. The individual and neighborhood problems that these representatives identify often will require action by the entire council. Therefore, we hypothesize that district representatives will bring questions concerning delivery of routine services to the council floor. The council member who has seen problems close at hand or who has heard about them from incensed constituents will be more likely to try to "do something" to solve problems and to do it publicly, where constituents can see that he is working for them.

We will test the following hypotheses concerning the impact of districts on council proceedings:

1. There will be greater and more overt controversy, indicated by increased proportions of non-unanimous votes and by increased disagreement in council discussions.
2. Increased conflict will be found in the following policy areas:
   a. redistribution and social services
   b. police and other protective services
   c. planning and zoning
   d. decision-making process.
3. Voting coalitions based on race, ethnicity, and district demographics will emerge.
4. The number and proportion of council discussions and votes devoted to routine services will increase.

POLICY OUTCOMES

Some pluralists and many district advocates would argue that once district systems are in place, minority representatives will achieve substantive policy gains that were impossible under at-large systems. However, as Karnig and Welch have stated, "proportionality [of council members] is an important step toward gaining power, but it is no guarantee that a substantial degree of power will be forthcoming".

(1980: 104) The extent of the impact that changing electoral structure has on policy outcomes depends largely on whether previously under-represented groups become a majority, a near-majority, or merely a distinctive minority on district councils. And, as Karnig and Welch suggest, (1980: 104–107) the greatest likelihood of council control for minorities is where they are, in fact, the majority group in a given city.

Equity does not equal control; if, for example, blacks do not comprise a council majority or do not have enough strength to bargain for partnership in winning coalitions, only marginal changes in substantive actions of local government may result from adoption of districts. On the other hand, increased symbolic benefits may be distributed to minority groups once district systems are in place regardless of their strength on district councils. As Edelman (1964) tells us, such benefits entail minimal costs and often result in diminished demands for substantive benefits.

We will test two somewhat dissonant policy hypotheses:

1. District advocates believe that the new structure has brought about improvements in their city.
2. Substantive changes in distribution of municipal facilities and services will be made only in cities where district elections allow previously underrepresented groups to gain majority or near majority status on council.

TESTING THE HYPOTHESES: SELECTION OF CITIES FOR COMPARATIVE CASE STUDIES

The fourteen hypotheses we have developed will be tested with data gathered over a two-year period in ten large cities that established districts during the past fifteen years and in a deviant-case city that moved toward at-large representation during the 1970s.

Much of what we know of urban political processes, generally, including the causes and effects of changes in the form of local representation, comes either from analysis of data from a large number of cities at a single time (for example, see Karnig, 1976; Robinson and Dye, 1978; Taebel, 1978; MacManus, 1978; Karnig and Welch, 1980; Eulau and Prewitt, 1973; Lineberry and Fowler, 1967; Clark, 1968), or from detailed, often insightful studies of individual cities (for example, Dahl, 1961; Lowi, 1964; Wirt, 1974; Rakove, 1975; Pressman and Wildavsky, 1973; Meltsner, 1971; Wolfinger, 1974; and Lineberry, 1977). From the aggregate analyses we get evidence of relationships which can be generalized to a wide range of urban places. The case studies, on the other hand, are rich in insights, especially concerning the contexts in which policy is made. The first approach is broad but somewhat shallow, the second deep but perhaps idiosyncratic. We have selected a middle ground between these approaches, hoping to combine rigor with richness in a comparative examination of a limited yet varied sample of large American cities.

The eleven cities included in this sample are Charlotte, Dallas, Des Moines, Fort Worth, Memphis, Montgomery, Peoria, Raleigh, Richmond, Sacramento and San Antonio. These are in no way a random sample of some larger population of cities; rather, they were chosen because they have common properties as well as differences crucial to our analysis. They are alike, with one exception, in that they are cities of 100,000 or more population that have experienced a change from at-large to district representation. Peoria is the exception, in that it is the only large American city to have changed to a more at-large system of representation in the 1970s. It did, however, change from at-large to district elections, if only briefly, during the 1960s. Peoria will provide a test as to whether changes we identify in the other locales result from greater district representation, or just more generally from structural change. Each of the cities, then, has a "district" period—including mixed systems which combine district and at-large seats—and an "at-large" period, the two possible values of the variable "form of representation."

The important differences among the eleven cities are both contextual and political. In terms of basic demographics, Table 2.1 shows a total population range between 122,000 and 844,000, with 1970 national rankings from eighth (Dallas) to 120th (Peoria) for the cities proper, and tenth (Dallas-Fort Worth) to 141st (Montgomery) for the SMSAs. Racial composition ranges from the "majority minority" cities of San Antonio and Richmond to Des Moines, which is 94 percent white (see Table 2.1). Des Moines and Peoria provide the opportunity to assess district efforts and consequences in the absence of race as a motivating factor. Our expectations concerning the effects of districts should hold for any geographically concentrated minority; since these midwestern cities include observable residential concentrations of less-affluent whites without the sizable black areas found in our southern cities, their inclusion allows us to test the accuracy of these expectations. Conversely, the inclusion of Sacramento and the Texas cities brings into our analysis the effect of district representation on the much less concentrated Spanish-speaking minority. Geographically, the cities are dispersed roughly according to the frequency of the change-to-districts movement, with nine of the eleven in Sunbelt states between Virginia and California.

Table 2.1. Sample City Characteristics

1970 pop (to nearest 1000)	City	Council Composition # Dist. Members	# AL Members	Community % Minority Blk/Asian	Spanish	Council changed from	Date of (D Election) Changes	Type of Change
727	San Antonio	10	1*	8	52	9 AL, mayor from council	1977	Justice Dept pressure: annexation
250	Richmond	9	0	42	—	9 AL, mayor from council	1977	Fedl. Court & Justice Dept; annexation
624	Memphis	7	6	40	—	5-member commission	1968	Referendum
133	Montgomery	9	0	34	—	3-member commission	1975	Referendum under Justice Dept. pressure
844	Dallas	8	3*	25	8	9 AL*	1975	Court order
241	Charlotte	7	4	31	—	7 AL	1977	Referendum
393	Fort Worth	8	1*	20	9	9 AL*	1977	Refereudum
257	Sacramento	8	2*	15	9	9 AL, mayor from council	1971	Referendum
122	Raleigh	5	3	23	—	7 AL, mayor from council	1972	Referencum
127	Peoria	5	3	11	—	AL, then 10 Dist.	1961/1973	Referendum
201	Des Moines	4	3	6	—	7 AL	1968	Referendum

*Includes mayor as voting member (but elected as mayor)

Politically, we are interested in the manner in which the change in electoral structure took place. There are essentially two categories of change, one in which change was implemented locally, through a referendum, and the other comprising those cities where districts were a response to pressure from the federal government. Such pressure may have been in the form of Justice Department "advice" that the change was necessary to bring the city into compliance with the Voting Act of 1965, or it may have been a Federal Court order. The cities selected for study include four cases of important federal government intervention, and six where the change to districts was largely the product of internal political dynamics.

We have tried to achieve a selection of cases that is broadly representative on the range of variables relevant to the district phenomenon, yet small enough to permit investigation of the contexts unique to each case. Rigorous quantitative analysis is provided by our files of council candidates, precincts, and interviews, while the comparative approach also enabled us to become knowledgeable in the political histories of our somewhat similar yet somewhat unique cities.

NOTES

1   Modern writers have developed this empirical distinction from its theoretical base in Edmund Burke's Speech to the Electors of Bristol (Burke, 1774).

3

Efforts to Adopt Districts

The process by which a group will attempt to change the structure of government is essentially determined by two factors. First, there are legal "rules of the game" provided by higher levels of government, or limitations of more fundamental documents such as constitutions. Second, to the degree that the rules allow for strategic options, group leaders must match the nature of their resources to the alternative that appears most likely to succeed.

In the United States, local government is an extension of the state. Such variation as is allowed in the structure of local institutions is clearly defined in state laws or constitutions, as is the process of change. If both district and at-large representation, or some combination thereof, are permitted by state legislation or constitutional provisions, there are commonly two procedures by which change from one form of representation to another can take place. The local council can itself decide to change its structure, with or without state ratification, or a referendum may be called; such referenda are based on council authorization or on the presentation of petitions signed by some minimal proportion of a city's registered voters.

Another level of government can become relevant to this process. Because of the tendency for at-large elections to result in less-than-proportionate representation for minorities, spokesmen for minority groups have frequently appealed for change directly to the federal government.

Examples of all these possible strategies, alone or in combination, appear in the experiences of our survey cities. In Chapter 1, with data from a national survey of cities, we considered the factors which might influence minority groups to replace at-large with district systems. Here we will first examine the strategic choices made in the sunbelt cities in that survey, then shift the focus to those cities which we have studied in depth, allowing state and federal constitutional constraints to be taken into consideration.

SOUTHERN CITY SURVEY

One-third of the 175 at-large southern cities in our survey of black-minority cities moved toward greater district representation during the 1970s, with another 22 percent experiencing unsuccessful district attempts. Table 3.1 is based on the 97 southern cities where efforts, successful or unsuccessful, toward district representation were reported. Looking first at the totals in the right-hand column, we find that most such efforts are local, based on referendum drives or local council action. Table 3.2 shows the relative success of the alternative strategies. These data must be interpreted cautiously, however. In the first place, the category "council action" includes only those cases where this was the ultimate form of action; district advocates who met defeat at the council level often tried alternative measures, and those cases are categorized by their final strategy. This explains the high rate of success for drives that ended with council action. Secondly, since each strategy was successful in some proportion of the cases reported, it is critical to our understanding of the process to identify the context in which a strategy is most likely to be successful.

We hypothesize that the most important aspect of the context is the relative size of a city's black population. If one assumes that district proponents are rational political actors, the high rate of success for referenda may reflect correct calculations as to the likelihood of mass support in each electoral setting. Table 3.1 shows the relationship between the percentage of black and the strategy ultimately employed by district advocates.

The referendum was clearly more popular where the black population was small, while appeals for federal intervention became more likely with an increase in the proportion of blacks. However, once the referen-

Table 3.1. Strategy of Change Toward District
Representation By Proportion Black of the Population

Strategy	Percentage Black			
	15–29.9	30–49.9	50 or greater	Total
Referendum	45%	34%	22%	38%
	(21)	(14)	(2)	(37)
Federal Court/	32	44	33	37
Justice Dept.	(15)	(18)	(3)	(36)
State Legislature or	11	2	44	10
Council Action	(5)	(1)	(4)	(10)
Petition/Discussion	13	20	0	14
only	(6)	(8)	(0)	(14)
Total:	100	100	100	100
	(47)	(41)	(9)	(97)

Significant at .01

dum strategy was chosen, its success was only weakly linked to the size of the black population; 66.7 percent (14/21) of the attempts succeeded where blacks comprised less than 30 percent of the city, compared to a 78.6 percent rate of success (11/14) where the black percentage was between 40 and 49.9 percent. There were two referenda in cities with black majorities, and both were successful.

Looking now at the cities where Hispanics were the largest minority group, we find a rather different pattern from the cities with a predominantly black minority. There is a most striking difference in the propensity of the two minorities to seek district representation: Attempts occurred in only 16 percent of the at-large sunbelt cities where Hispanics comprise the relevant minority. Sixty-one percent of the eighteen district

Table 3.2. Percentage of Successful Attempts at Change Toward
Districts by Strategy and Proportion Black of the Population

Strategy	Percent of Minority Population			
	15–30	31–49	50 or greater	Total
Referendum	67%	79%	100%	73%
Federal Court/ Justice Dept.	67%	44%	0%	50%
State Legislature or Council Action	100%	13%	100%	100%

N's same as in Table 2.1

efforts in Hispanic cities were referenda, while only 11 percent involved litigation. In contrast, referenda and legal actions were employed in almost equal proportions in black-minority cities. The referendum was not a particularly successful strategy for Hispanics, as only 27 percent of the elections resulted in adoption of districts. In the black cities, however, over 70 percent of the referenda were successful, compared to half the legal actions.

In summary, blacks and Hispanics have not perceived the solution to representational inequities in the same manner, nor have they been successful with the same strategies. Blacks are much more likely to prefer districts as a remedy, undoubtedly reflecting their generally greater geographic concentration. This difference is not just academic in a city with sizable populations of both blacks and Hispanics. The problem of differing minority preferences reappears in the case studies that follow.

ELEVEN-CITY STUDY

As shown in Table 1.3, the same pattern was evident in the methods of change used in the eleven cities of our comparative study. This pattern is not difficult to understand; where minorities are small, they present no threat of government "takeover," and often can gain the support of some portion of the white population to form a voting majority. But the closer the minority population is to being a majority of voters, the more salient race becomes. Change by referendum becomes unlikely, and minorities look to the federal government for help.

The Legal Basis for Federal Intervention

We will now examine in greater detail the rules of the game that have permitted federal intervention, and see them applied to the four cities in our study with largest minority populations, Richmond, San Antonoio, Montgomery, and Dallas. (Although Memphis ranks among the cities with the greatest minority poportions, the move to districts there took place in 1968, in a different legal and political climate. That case will be examined separately.)

Legal precedents for court challenges to at-large systems as inherently biased against minorities are found in Supreme Court decisions on legislative apportionment and multimember state legislative districts (Claunch and Hallman, 1978: 1). In *Baker* v. *Carr* (369 U.S. 186, 1962) the Supreme Court entered the "political thicket," accepting the question of apportionment as justiciable. Thus encouraged, groups perceiving themselves as underrepresented in local government have used two approaches: judicial or administrative (Justice Department) redress under the Voting Rights Act of 1965; and challenges to the constitutionality of at-large voting under the Fourteenth and Fifteenth amendments.[1]

The Voting Rights Act of 1965 was the major legislative victory of the civil rights movement in the 1960s. Its regulations applied to states or localities which had previously employed literacy tests as prerequisites to voter registration and had recorded registration or turnouts of less than 50 percent of voting-age population in November 1964. Section 5 of the act was relevant to local representation, as it required covered jurisdictions to submit proposed changes in voting and representation to the Attorney General or the U.S. District Court for the District of Columbia for approval.[2] In rejecting several challenges to the 1965 Act, the Supreme Court upheld its constitutionality (*South Carolina* v. *Katzenbach*, 383 U.S. 301, 1966), and interpreted it to cover almost any change in electoral laws, including municipal annexations (*Perkins* v. *Matthews*, 400 U.S. 379, 1971).

An important limitation on the use of Section 5 by minorities was that it applied only to jurisdictions meeting the conditions of overt voter discrimination described above. Even in covered jurisdictions, the act had no effect on at-large systems already in place; it applied only to attempts to dilute minority voting strength. In the cases under consideration here, it is the application of the Act to annexations that is directly relevant. Houston beat back a constitutional challenge to its at-large council, only to be forced to adopt districts in order to win Justice Department approval of an annexation. Similar circumstances prevailed in Richmond and San Antonio.

Richmond. The adoption of districts by the city of Richmond grew out of interrelated trends common to American cities in the 1960s: The erosion of the central city tax base, immigration of black residents, and out-migration of whites. Early in the decade, the city administration began to lay ground-work for extending Richmond's limits through annexation, ostensibly for fiscal and planning purposes. Such an annexation did eventually take place, in 1970, but it brought on years of litigation as to the city's intent at the time of the action: Was it still based on a primary concern for fiscal health, as city officials maintained? Justice William Brennan supported the contrary explanation of Richmond's black ledership, charging in his dissent to the decision in *Richmond* v. *United States* (422 U.S. 358) that "those legitimate goals had been pushed into the background by the unseemly haste of the white political establishment to protect and solidify its position of power." Richmond's black population had grown from 42 percent of the city in 1960 to 52 percent in 1970. With annexation completed in time for the 1970 elections, but before the publication of the federal census, blacks again comprised just 42 percent of the city's total population. The Crusade for Voters of Richmond, the major black political organization, filed suit in federal court to block the annexation, and won an injunction in 1972 barring the city from holding further elections pending judgment on the case. There were to be no local elections in Richmond until 1977. The Richmond case reached the Supreme Court in 1975, resulting in a 5–3 decision that southern cities can alter their racial composition by annexation as long as their motives are legitimate and blacks enjoy a proportional share of power (*Richmond* v. *U.S., supra*). The case was remanded to the lower courts with instructions to develop an appropriate system of district representation.

In order to maintain its annexed areas, and to regain the right to hold local elections, the city agreed to a Justice Department proposal whereby the nine-member at-large city council would be replaced by a council with nine district seats. Four districts would be predominantly white, four would be at least 63 percent black, and a ninth "swing" ward would be 59 percent white. The Council's two black members opposed this plan, saying they would continue to fight the annexation unless a plan were approved which guaranteed five black seats. Despite this opposition, the city presented the plan to the state legislature for charter revision, and then returned it to the federal courts. A three-judge panel upheld the annexation in August of 1976, and in November of that year Judge Robert Merhige lifted the ban against local elections.

The Richmond district plan proved not to be as racially balanced as the participants had judged. Some black leaders thought they had been presented a plan for continued white dominance, and wondered, as the city's population inched toward majority black, why they should not have held on to the at-large system that had worked so well for the previous white majority. To everyone's surprise, the "swing" district turned out to be safely black, and the first council elected under districts (in 1977) included a five-member black majority. Voting as a bloc on organizational matters, the five blacks elected Henry L. Marsh III as the first black mayor in modern Richmond history. The 1978 election produced virtually the same result, and black control of Richmond seemed assured.

To say that leaders of the white community were distressed at the outcome of district elections, and chagrined at Mayor Marsh's ability to marshall the black membership behind him on crucial votes, is to understate the emotional level of Richmond politics. In 1980, one black incumbent was challenged in a concerted effort, as the white political movement known as TOPS (Teams of Progress) channeled support to her white opponent. Disappointed again in the narrow defeat of their candidate, white political leaders took other actions. The Richmond Independent Taxpayers Association attempted through two referenda to limit the city's taxing power, while the white council members sought to gain leverage by blocking adoption of the budget, which required more than a simple majority for adoption.

Taking advantage of the requirement to redistrict based on 1980 population figures, Mayor Marsh presented a plan to redraw the city's districts in a fashion that would render black control more secure. (According to the 1980 census figures, even including the annexations that led to districts, Richmond is now 51 percent black). Not surprisingly, the plan was adopted 5-4, and, in an ironic turn of events, white citizens used the Voting Rights Act as the basis for a plea to the Justice Department to reject the redistricting as discriminatory to white voters in its guarantee of a black majority.

The effort to sway the Justice Department included a barrage of 3,000 letters and the appearance at Justice of a delegation including the four white council members, prominent businessmen, and, to test the new winds of the Reagan administration, "two of Virginia's most prominent GOP fundraisers." Their special influence was to no avail: Assistant Attorney General William Reynolds of the Department's Civil Rights Division determined that the plan was drawn "in a conscientious and fair manner," and that it was an accurate reflection of the continued increase in Richmond's black population (*Washington Post*, September 1, 1981).

The seemingly permanent split in the Richmond council was softened in the May, 1982, election of the fourth district council. A black middle-school principal, Dr. Roy A. West, narrowly defeated a member of Mayor Marsh's coalition. West received 53 percent of the district's vote, with a majority in just five of its nine precincts; three of these were the only predominantly white precincts in the district. West had pointedly pledged his independence of the existing council's coalitions. At the same time, two candidates challenged former manager Leidinger for his council seat. They charged that he had contributed to council divisiveness because of bitterness over his having been fired. Leidinger, however, beat back the challenge, winning by a 60 percent majority.

West's campaign had drawn considerable attention, and both factions were courting him. Ultimately, the TOP group could make the best offer: their support in the selection of a mayor. West kept both groups in suspense until the last minute. At the first meeting of the new council, in July, 1982, the four votes of the "black bloc" had been cast for Marsh, the four white votes for West. According to the *Richmond Times-Dispatch*, West then "made himself mayor by pausing dramatically and then speaking his name." This pivotal position, enhanced by West's alphabetic rank on the council roster, suggests a continued position of strength for the incumbent in the structurally weak mayor's role in Richmond. West promised to use his advantage much less predictably than did Marsh. However, there is no reason to believe that the basic council divisions have been reduced as a consequence: West voted with the white council members against the Marsh bloc in the first seventeen split votes in which he participated; thus, although the council voting split crosses the color line, it is as predictable as before. (Washington *Post*, August 30, 1983)

District representation has been one aspect of a bitter struggle over control of the Richmond government. It is an awesome analytic challenge to sort the causes and effects of districts from the racially based turmoil that has been the rule in Richmond for twelve years. In other cities, antagonists over districts have come to feel that perhaps the difference in representational structure is not, after all, so momentous. In Richmond the issue has been central to the struggle for power, but proposals from the white business leadership to move away from the district plan were moved to the back burner while they assessed their prospects under the West administration.

San Antonio. Mexican-Americans are the predominant minority in San Antonio, composing 52 percent of the population in 1970 and 54 percent in 1980. Blacks make up another 8 percent. Yet the city council had long been white-dominated, or more particularly, under the control of the Good Government League (Lineberry 1977: 55–57). This political organization chose slates, and backed them financially under an at-large system in which a candidate had to file for a specific seat, and win that seat by an absolute majority. Although the GGL had included some blacks and Mexican-Americans on its slates in the 1970s, those slated constituted definite minorities on the council and had to take positions acceptable to the majority of San Antonio voters.[3]

Minority leaders in San Antonio may not have been aware of the Richmond case, but they were sensitized to the possibility of federal intervention by successful challenges in the early 1970s to multimember districts in the Texas Legislature. In 1973, the Supreme Court declared that multimember districts in Dallas and Bexar County (which includes San Antonio) were unconstitutional (*White* v. *Regester*, 412 U.S. 767).

That same year, the GGL came temporarily unglued, allowing nonslated candidates to win five of the nine council seats. This antiestablishment council appointed a charter revision commission. That body developed a proposal to expand the council to eleven members, with four (including the mayor) to be elected at-large and seven from districts. This plan was placed on the November, 1974, ballot, and was defeated by a margin of 52 to 48 percent. The vote was ethnically polarized, with Mexican-American wards supporting the plan by margins of two to one, and other areas opposing it by the same margin.

The Voting Rights Act of 1975 expanded the application of its predecessors from denial of voting rights based on race (Fifteenth Amendment) to any denial of equality in voting (Fourteenth Amendment). Between 1972 and 1974, San Antonio had annexed thirteen outlying areas that were only 23 percent Mexican-American. In April 1976, the city was informed by the Justice Department that the annexation would not be allowed unless San Antonio adopted a single-member-district plan for choosing the council. San Antonio thus became the first city without a large black population to run afoul of the Voting Rights Act as a result of annexation.

The Justice announcement set off a heated debate. Some local elites were ready to challenge this federal intervention into local government, but others were more aware of the direct and indirect costs, such as deannexations and forestalled elections, of a court suit. A Mexican-American political organization, Communities Organized for Public Services (COPS), had already begun to challenge GGL dominance, and now supported the Justice Department suggestion. By an 8–1 vote, the city council drew up a ten-district plan as a referendum proposal.

In January, 1977, a bare 51 percent of the voters approved the new district plan, under the same conditions of voter polarization as in 1974. Perhaps because the battle was not as protracted as in Richmond, and did not involve a court order, the GGL's reaction to defeat was one of acquiescence. The organization's leadership announced that it would no longer slate and endorse candidates, and slating efforts and formal coalitions ended with the change to districts.

The first district elections, as in Richmond, resulted in a "majority minority," council consisting of five Mexican-Americans, one black, and four "Anglos." However, in 1979, a Mexican-American member from an ethnically mixed district lost his seat in a run-off election, and the balance shifted again to an Anglo majority. Ethnic-based coalitions became less salient on the 1979 council, and political stability was increased in 1981 with the election of Henry Cisneros as the first Mexican-American mayor of a major U.S. city. Cisneros had in past years been part of the GGL slate; although he asserted independence in his council voting behavior even on the at-large council, he still inspired confidence in the wealthy precincts as well as among working-class Mexican-American. He won a landslide mandate of 62 percent in a record turnout for a local election, carrying some Spanish-speaking precincts by 30–1, but almost winning in the non-Spanish north side as well. According to the *New York Times* (April 6, 1981), Cisneros "has assiduously tried to build bridges between the Mexican-Americans . . . and the non-Hispanic establishment." His election thus symbolizes a significant reduction of tension in San Antonio politics.

There is no indication that district representation will reappear as an issue in San Antonio, even though the context of change is strikingly similar to that of Richmond.

Dallas. The limitation of the Voting Rights Act to *changes* in voting procedures could leave ongoing discriminatory procedures untouched. In the absence of change or proposed change, a discrimination charge must take the form of a lawsuit in federal court; the constitutional basis for such suits would still be the Fourteenth or Fifteenth Amendments, but there is no automatic "trigger" mechanism to bring the Department of Justice into action. While these suits can be filed anywhere in the country, in fact almost all important challenges have arisen in the Fifth Judicial Circuit, which covers the southernmost tier of states from Florida to Texas.[4] Judges sitting in that circuit have been willing to presume the widespread use of at-large elections for discriminatory purposes. The Fifth District Court has looked at questions of at-large bias in light of Supreme Court rulings on the use of multimember districts in state legislatures, as in *White v. Regester* (referred to above as instrumental in sensitizing minorities to this issue in San Antonio and in Texas generally). The overall thrust of the Fifth District rulings was that it is sufficient to show discriminatory *effect*, rather than *intent*, to demonstrate an unconstitutional dilution of voting strength.

In Dallas, the form of council representation was under litigation for nearly the entire decade of the 1970s. Under at-large elections in the 1960s, black candidates built up impressive majorities in inner-city precincts, but lost citywide unless they were able to win the endorsement of the Citizens' Charter Association (Claunch and Hallman 1978: 2). The CCA was formed in 1936 as the Dallas Citizens' Council, with membership limited to 250 executives from the largest corporations and banks in the city. The organization drafted slates of candidates, and provided sufficient campaign funds to insure their election (*New York Times*, May 10, 1981).

The first constitutional challenge of Dallas's at-large system was dismissed in 1971 by a Federal District judge, but the Fifth Circuit Court of Appeals vacated and remanded the case to the district court the next year (*Lipscomb* v. *Johnson*, 459 F. 2nd 335). While the challenge was working its way back through the federal court process, the *Regester* decision was announced. The district court now found the at-large system to be unconstitutional, but offered the city council an opportunity to prepare an acceptable plan. The council then proposed a mixed system based on eight districts and three at-large seats. This plan was accepted in 1975 by the district court, which noted that Dallas's Mexican-American population was too small and dispersed to benefit from wards, and might have more impact as the swing vote in the at-large contests. The Fifth Circuit Court of Appeals rejected the council proposal for violating what it saw as a Supreme Court mandate to apply single-member districts in any court-ordered plan. The city then appealed to the Supreme Court, which upheld the District court's approval of the 8–3 plan. In *Wise* v. *Lipscomb* (437 U.S. 535, 1978), the Supreme Court ruled that the 8–3 plan was a legislative enactment of the council, not a court-mandated plan, and thus exempt from its single-member-district rule.

The legality of the 8–3 plan was not settled by this decision, however. On remand, the Court of Appeals determined that, since the 8–3 plan had been declared a legislative enactment by the Supreme Court, it was at that point covered by Section 5 of the Voting Rights Act, and required preclearance by the District Court of the District of Columbia or the Attorney General. For his part, the Attorney General saw the plan as dilutive, since blacks would probably control three seats on an all-district council, but just two seats under the 8–3 arrangement.

The city next sought a declaratory judgement for the plan from the District Court of the District of Columbia, which, however, ruled that a trial would be necessary to settle the issue. At the same time the minority plaintiffs continued their offensive against the 8–3 plan in another lawsuit. In *Heggins* v. *City of Dallas* (469 F. Supp. 739, N.D. Tex., 1979), they asked that the city be prevented from holding council elections until preclearance was obtained. A federal judge panel issued an injunction postponing the 1979 elections until the matter was resolved. The minority plaintiffs proposed an all-district plan, to which the city responded by redrawing district lines to provide three districts with large minority populations. In November, 1979, the Justice Department approved the city's proposal, and the "1979" elections were held in January, 1980.

In the meantime, the District of Columbia district court had decided that the case pending before them, based on the previous district lines, was now moot, since the two plans were different and the more recent had been approved by the Justice Department.

The protracted legal battle over the Dallas plan reflected changing standards and legal situations, but it also resulted from the conflicting interests of the two minority groups involved, one concentrated in residence patterns, the other dispersed. Although Mexican-Americans share with blacks a sense of underrepresentation, they are only 8 percent of the population (compared to the 25 percent that is black), and do not comprise a majority in any of the eight districts. Thus, some of them have argued that their chances for proportionate representation might be greatest in a mixed district/at-large system; their argument has been accepted by federal judges at some points in the judicial process, and rejected at others.

The 8–3 plan had been put into effect in Dallas by council action for the 1975 election. In April, 1976, it was approved by referendum and incorporated into the city charter. Thus, the mixed system has governed the last four council elections in Dallas, even as it has been under continuous judicial scrutiny. In these elections, Dallas has regularly elected two black members, and in one case a Mexican-American; neighborhood groups and their endorsements have emerged as significant in Dallas under district elections.

On the other hand, minority leaders have been rather disappointed at the results of their long struggle for more equitable council representation, because now that they are present on the council, it seems that the center of policymaking has shifted from the council to the mayor and city manager. Both these officials are viewed as operating independently of the council, often presenting them with *fait accompli* decisions for their ratification. The current mayor, Jack Evans, was a relatively unknown businessman who monopolized the business community's financial resources in his campaign; he was swept into office with a 72 percent majority in an election that drew only 17 percent of the voters (*New York Times*, May 10, 1981). Both he and his predecessor are seen as representatives of the elite that has controlled Dallas in recent history, and City Manager George Schrader, who resigned in 1981, was openly hostile to the district plan. A Coalition of Minority Representation has emerged, showing that black and Mexican-American leaders are not satisfied with their level of influence in Dallas politics. As a result of the 1980 census, the city drew up new district boundaries, still under the 8–3 plan, that would provide two predominantly black districts and one with a large concentration, but not a majority, of Mexican-American residents. Black members of the council challenged the plan, arguing for a third predominantly black district, and warning of further litigation if the Justice Department does not object to the plan.

In summary, the 8–3 plan was one developed by, and defended by, the city administration against minority, mostly black, demands for a purely district system. There is no sign that any group will attempt to return to a more at-large system in Dallas, but the city's blacks and Mexican-Americans continue to press both for more districts and for other means of increasing their influence in decision making. In the process, the two minority groups are frequently at odds with each other, leaving a complex trail of political and legal maneuvers.

Mobile, The Bolden Case and the Extension of the Voting Rights Act. The constitutional questions raised in the Dallas case were not resolved there. In Justice Rehnquist's concurring opinion in *Wise* v. *Lipscomb*, the question was explicitly left open. Noting that the state-legislature context in *White* v. *Regester* may not necessarily be relevant in municipal government situations, but that that particular issue was not addressed in *Wise* v. *Lipscomb*, Rehnquist observed that

> We need not today consider whether relevant constitutional distinctions may be drawn in this area between a state legislature and a municipal government. I write only to point out that the possibility of such distinctions has not been foreclosed by today's decision.[5]

With the settlement of the Dallas case, the question of districts and minority representation has been focused on Mobile, Alabama. A district Court ruled in 1976 that the at-large election of Mobile's three-person city commission diluted the voting power of the city's blacks. In 1978 the fifth Circuit Court of Appeals supported the district court decision, reaffirming its position that a system is unconstitutional if its effect, intended or not, is to dilute (*Bolden* v. *City of Mobile*, 571 F. 2nd 238).

The Fifth Circuit position was firmly repudiated by the Supreme Court (*City of Mobile* v. *Bolden*, 48 L.W. 4436, 1980); this, however, was a decision that did not build on a majority-supported opinion. Justices Stewart, Burger, Powell, and Rehnquist declared that discriminatory purpose in the creation of an at-large system must be demonstrated for the system to be rejected by the Court. Although the Mobile decision appeared tentative due to this lack of consensus, its immediate effect was to discourage further constitutional challenges of systems already in place. Intent is much more difficult to prove in government decisions than is the effect of such decisions. This observation was behind the inclusion in the 1982 extension of the Voting Rights Act of a change in Section 2 permitting challenges to any electoral procedure *"which results* in a denial of abridgement" of a citizen's vote because of race.

After the Mobile decision it appeared likely that Dallas would be the last major city to adopt districts under the threat of federal intervention. In June, 1982, however, the issue was reopened by the twenty-five-year extension of the Act with its revised section 2. Mobile and other at-large cities are seeing renewed challenges to their form of representation.

DISTRICTS BY LOCAL DECISION

Minorities cannot change local political structures without someone's help. But the smaller the minority population, the less threatening it is, and the greater the likelihood of a local alliance.

Under the Shadow of Federal Intervention

In the middle range of minority proportions we find several cities where neither the Constitution nor the Voting Rights Act were overtly evoked, but where awareness of those possibilities guided majority leaders or groups to a "local" decision in favor of districts.

Fort Worth. Fort Worth began electing its city council from districts in 1977 without significant strife or animosity.[6] Several factors account for this. First, much of the resistance to district representation had been weakened in earlier conflicts. Second, citizens were aware of the effects of districts in the Texas legislature and cities such as Dallas. Third, voters were given a clear choice: Either they maintained a council elected entirely at large or one chosen from eight single-member districts. Finally, the city's political and economic leadership could not agree on a single plan.

No black served on the city council until 1967, and only two were elected in the next ten years. Chicanos had an even more disappointing track record: None were elected under the at-large system of representation. Although there were Mexican-American candidates in three of the six elections from 1965 to 1975, their best showing was 25 percent of the vote.

Attacks on the at-large city council began in the early seventies and became part of a black and liberal white challenge to the so-called establishment of utilities, downtown banks, and the local newspaper.

Although the major battles in this conflict were not fought over the at-large city council, they weakened the "establishment" enough that it offered little opposition when voters adopted the change in 1975.

In addition to attacking their opponents in the courts, the liberal coalition argued from the experiences of other elected bodies to support their campaign for districts. They pointed, for instance, to minority gains in the Texas House as a benefit of single-member districts. They also argued that serious costs to community harmony and to a progressive image would result from a failure to adopt districts. As evidence, they cited Dallas's decade-long battle in court defending its mixed system.

The ultimate effect of the prodistrict campaign was division within the "establishment" ranks. Because of the lengthening history of court challenges nationally, and the potential effects of the Voting Rights Act, many supporters of the at-large system sensed the inevitability of districts and either endorsed the change or offered no opposition.

The charter revision campaign in Fort Worth was quite uneventful. After extensive review, the Charter Revision Committee recommended a plan with five members elected by district and three members and the mayor elected at-large. The city council disregarded this suggestion and voted 5–4 to submit a charter amendment which provided for a mayor elected at large and eight members chosen from districts. There is a great deal of speculation regarding the reason for the council's action. Many district advocates accused their council opponents of submitting the 8–1 plan because they expected it to lose.

There was very little open campaigning on the district plan or the other eighteen charter amendments on the April 1975 ballot. The only visible group in the election was the League of Women Voters, which conducted a campaign of public meetings, fliers, and media announcements in favor of the district plan. The proponents also enjoyed the endorsement of the *Star-Telegram*.

Fort Worth voters approved the district plan by less than 200 votes out of more than 30,000 cast. At the same time, they rejected by over 6,000 votes a proposal to elect council members to four-year, staggered terms. The vote for districts was highly related to the proportion minority (black and Mexican-American) population in each precinct ($r = .84$). The relationship between vote for districts and average house value ($r = -.52$) virtually disappeared when controlled for proportion minority (partial correlation $= -.03$). However, although reaction to the proposal was sharply divided ethnically at the precinct level, the vote was almost evenly divided in most of the predominantly white precincts, and was slightly prodistrict in some of them. The overall majority for the proposal and the high statistical relationship with ethnic identity was insured by uniform majorities of 80 percent or more in the heavily black precincts.

The first council chosen from districts in 1977 was quite a departure from its predecessors. Its eight members included two blacks, a Mexican-American, and two liberal whites.

After three elections under districts, the original opponents and skeptics, notably present and former city administrators, argue that the quality of council members has declined and that log rolling among members prevents the council from taking a larger view of the city's problems. But another group which is not altogether happy with the change includes some of the original proponents, who have now concluded that districts did not make any difference. They argue that the same groups who dominated previous councils have been able to reassert themselves through their campaign contributions and their backing of conservative black candidates. As evidence, they cite an increasing power of incumbency and declining citizen interest in local matters as indicated by lower turnout.

Montgomery. The capital of Alabama has been the site of civil rights dramas that would seem to dwarf questions of local representation. This is the city where Rosa Parks refused to give up her seat on the bus, and where Martin Luther King, Jr., began his political career. It also provided the stage for George C. Wallace to defy the federal government and launch his own well-known entry into national politics. Finally, it is the home of Federal District Judge Frank M. Johnson, Jr., whose judicial activism and frequent conflict with Governor Wallace kept Montgomery in the headlines. What is surprising is that Montgomery's move to districts was only tangentially involved with black voting rights.

Before the 1970s, Montgomery was governed by a three-member commission, with one of the three positions designated as mayor. Mayors such as Earl James (1963–1970) were elected on the basis of solid ''establishment'' support, following selection by business leaders and newspaper owners. The same caucuses usually produced the local state legislative delegation which then worked closely with the mayor and other commissioners. Economic development in the 1960s, however, brought a new leadership element into local politics; this group included radio and television station owners, and businessmen newly arrived in the city, especially those in real estate and development.

Mayor James provoked a loss of faith in his leadership, principally by allowing unionization of city employees. He failed to mount an effective reelection campaign in 1970, and was beaten in a primary run-off election by an insurance agent who had the backing of some of the new business interests. The winner, however, proceeded to get his own campaign in trouble by promising to stop urban renewal projects in the city. Business leaders who felt they needed a more reliable candidate approached James Robinson, a businessman who had moved to Montgomery from Georgia. With Robinson's consent they mounted a petition campaign that put him on the general election ballot, and then supported his successful campaign.

As mayor, Robinson wanted to establish firm control over the city administration, and soon became frustrated with the commission system. In one important challenge, the other commissioners sought to maintain their support among the firemen and police officers by approving pay increases for these employees that exceeded the budget. They also were maintaining practices that by modern norms could only be considered corrupt, including provisions of free gravel and paving on private property for prominent supporters, and allowing city garage personnel to use supplies for private work. Robinson succeeded in holding his commission colleagues responsible for a subsequent tax increase that he tied to the salary issue, and linked the continuing petty corruption with the commission system.

In order to obtain the kind of centralized decision-making power he wanted, Mayor Robinson developed a proposal for a mayor-council system. The plan had to provide for districts, however, both to win support for it among the black population, and, more directly, because Alabama was a covered jurisdiction under the Voting Rights Act. At Robinson's urging, the state legislature voted in 1974 to permit a change to a strong mayor and a council of nine district representatives if such an arrangement were approved in a local referendum. Although a campaign in opposition to the change was organized by one of the other commissioners, Robinson expressed surprise that the measure evoked as little controversy as it did; an obvious result, after all, would be the election of blacks to city office for the first time in this century. The racial issue was raised by extremists such as the Ku Klux Klan, but was not developed effectively by more credible opponents. On the other hand, black leaders supported the proposal enthusiastically, especially because Robinson's opponents were linked to a simultaneious effort to gerrymander state legislative districts.

The referendum passed by the slim margin of 52 to 48 percent. At first impression, the results by precinct do not reflect racial voting; there was no correlation between the percentage of a precinct's population that was black and the proportion of the vote for districts ($r = .06$). There was, however, a relationship between the average house value in a precinct (our usual census-based surrogate measure of income) and the vote for districts; the Pearson's coefficient in this case was .54, increasing to .65 when controlled for race. Heavy votes in favor were recorded in the highest-income white precincts, with more moderate support in black precincts. Low-income white precincts showed the heaviest opposition, with only 16 percent in favor of districts in one of them. Thus, adoption of districts in Montgomery was characterized not by racial polarization, but by a coalition of upper-income whites and blacks against lower-income whites. It is not unreasonable to assume that the issue of race was most salient among those whites whom classical southern social patterns would predict to behave in that manner.

Most of the attention to the difference in Montgomery's local government since the change in structure has focused on the office of mayor. Compared to the commission government it replaced, the mayor-council system has a clear chain of command, and that seems to overshadow the introduction of districts and of blacks to the council. Although critics can be found who fault the district system for introducing parochialism and council divisions along racial lines, there has been no organized effort to reconsider the district system in Montgomery.

Blurring the Racial Issue: Downtown-Neighborhood Conflicts

In the preceding cases of local initiative, successful efforts at adopting districts came as a result of actions by political or business leaders. Such advocates did not benefit in any consistent manner from district representation, but in order to modify the decision-making process without incurring racial strife, districts were a necessary ingredient in the proposals they developed. Our next category of cases includes cities where pressures for change in form of representation were from middle-class groups wishing to diffuse political powe, and where, consequently, incumbent leadership generally opposed structural change.

Charlotte. Charlotte had ward elections until the late 1940s. After World War II, the city obtained a charter change from the state legislature under conditions similar to Richmond's: A black candidate for council had come close to being elected from the ward in which black voters were concentrated. The at-large system thus implemented remained in effect with no challenge until the mid-1970s, when newly organized neighborhood groups began to perceive a lack of responsiveness from what they saw as a council dominated by downtown businessmen.

One immediate cause of discontent in white areas was federally imposed school busing. The greatest animosity engendered by this event broke out along racial lines. Still, some less-affluent whites were also resentful of civic leaders who urged peaceful acceptance of the law of the land, but sent their own children to private schools, and developed desegregation plans that spared upper-class neighborhoods from busing. Although this grievance was focused on the Board of Education, it was soon followed by city council approval of a scattered-site public housing plan in which scatter was limited to middle- and lower-income areas. In addition, community activists in black and low-income white areas saw a lack of political influence in the assignment to their side of town of throughways, the airport, and a sewage treatment plant, with a complementary lack of more desirable facilities and services.

All of these points were mentioned in interviews with activists as factors leading to the formation of a neighborhood-based movement aimed at gaining effective voice in local decision making.

In 1977, an umbrella organization called Neighborhoods United presented the council with a request for district representation, and supported council candidates who promised to vote for such a system. When the district concept was norrowly rejected by the council, Neighborhoods, United, operating through its twenty constituent organizations, drew up a plan for a mixed district/at-large system, and sponsored a successful petition calling for a referendum on the issue.

The mayor, most civic leaders, and a majority of the council expressed opposition to the plan. They did not, however, mount an organized or systematic campaign against it, nor were there any formal statements of opposition through such institutions as the Chamber of Commerce. In hindsight, several opponents attributed their inaction to complacency: They underestimated the determination and support of their new rivals. The neighborhood groups, on the other hand, although active with varying degrees of vigor, sponsored several public debates and, more importantly, organized door-to-door "get out the vote" drives.

District representation was approved by the barest of margins, 50.1 percent. Data by precinct show a mean "yes" vote of 55 percent, ranging from 24.6 to 97.9 percent. In the same election, a science museum was approved by 53.4 percent of the votes, and an arts center by 52.7 percent. The museum and art center can be viewed as traditional "public-regarding" issues, useful for comparison with the district vote.[7]

If blacks and working-to-middle class whites perceived the at-large system as biased against their interests, both groups should have supported the district plan. Such a coalition is in fact rare in local politics in any region;[8] it was particularly unlikely in Charlotte because of the struggle over court-ordered school busing.

Aggregate analysis in the Charlotte case shows that the vote was clearly split on the basis of income and race, in a way markedly different from the "public-regarding" issues of the arts center and science museum, or earlier structural-change referenda on city-county consolidation and on partisan local elections. The neighborhood organizations emerged as an important new factor determining the outcome of this election. Table 3.3 shows that lower-income white precincts joined with predominantly black precincts in giving district representation its margin of victory. On previous referenda, the vote in black precincts was more like that of upper-income white precincts than it was of lower-income white areas; this pattern was reversed in the case of districts. It is possible that the relationship between the presence of a neighborhood organization and support for districts is spurious; however, by comparing the difference in voting returns for lower-income white precincts with and without organizations, it is clear that there is no major difference between them on other recent issues. If we assume that the two groups are samples of a larger population, and calculate the F ratio on the difference between them on each issue, the difference is significant only in the case of the district vote, the only one in which the neighborhood organizations were involved.

On other issues, blacks tended to vote with upper-income whites and against lower- and middle-income whites. This is the classic urban voting pattern described by Banfield and Wilson (1963:35). But on the question of district representation, we find a unique voting coalition of blacks and lower and middle-income whites. Perhaps the most striking evidence for the novelty of this combination lies in the fact that both the Wallace vote in the 1976 Democratic presidential primary and the percentage of black registration in all precincts are strongly and directly related to district plan vote (Pearson's $r = .59$ and $.82$), even though there is a strong inverse relationship $(- .66)$ between Wallace vote and black registration in all precincts.

The first council under the new plan was elected in 1977. Within a year, there were rumors that opponents of districts, mindful of their narrow defeat in the referendum, would draw up a petition for another referendum on the issue. Mayor Kenneth Harris, whose single term was marked by an inability to work with the council, appointed a Charter Review Commission that district representatives and neighborhood activists saw as a vehicle to abolish districts. Their challenge came in more immediate fashion, however. Shortly after the 1979 election, district opponents went into action. Petitions for a new referendum were circulated with little fanfare, and only after opponents had secured the necessary signatures and had seen the date set for balloting did they emerge as an

Table 3.3. Voting Returns in Recent Local Referenda in Charlotte, by Precinct Percentage Averages

Issue position	A. Black[a] Precincts (16)	B. With Neighborhood organization (11)	C. No Neighborhood organization (37)	D. Upper-Income White Precincts (14)
For district representation (1977)	84.8	60.5 (.0022)[c]	46.3	39.3
For partisan local elections (1975)	50.7	49.9 (.1263)	53.3	55.1
For city/county consolidation (1971)	60.0	28.3 (.9014)	27.5	38.4
For bonds to build cultural center (1977)	76.6	42.3 (.3046)	46.7	50.3

aDefined as those precincts with 50 percent or more registered voters who are black. The cutoff point may seem arbitrary, but residential location is sufficiently segregated that shifting the exact point makes little difference: If a black precinct is defined as 30 percent or more black, there is only one more "black" precinct than under the 50 percent criterion.

bLower income precincts are defined as those with an average house value of less than $16,000 according to the 1970 census.

cSignificance of variance between columns B and C based on the F-ratio. Strictly speaking, calculation of a significance level is inappropriate here, because these are not samples of some definable larger population. Significance levels are presented here as *if they were* derived from sample statistics, to demonstrate the importance of the percentage difference in voting on various issues.

organization, the Better Way Committee. The old coalition of neighborhood and black groups reappeared as Citizens to Keep Districts. Thus, for the first time, the district issue in Charlotte saw organizations mobilized on each side.

The petition had been drawn up so as to return the city to an all at-large system. However, the author died in January, 1981, and new leadership saw the referendum's chances as better with some provision for districts. Saddled with the referendum's wording, they campaigned on a promise to return to a mixed system with a greater proportion of at-large representation once the existing system had been displaced.

This awkward electoral proposal no doubt contributed to the decisive defeat of the at-large initiative. It received a majority vote only in the two most affluent districts, also the principal source of the at-large petition signatures. The bare margin of victory achieved by the neighborhood coalition in 1977 had become a clear mandate for districts in 1981.

Raleigh. To a greater degree than in Charlotte, the Raleigh district movement was a product of an emerging neighborhood movement in middle-class white areas. The grievances are strikingly similar in the two North Carolina cities: Federally imposed school busing stimulated overt resentment against the "downtown establishment," which led to coordinated efforts to stop construction of throughways and public housing projects in all but the more affluent districts.

The community activists representing the aggrieved Raleigh neighborhoods numbered less than a dozen. They presented a petition for districts to the city council in late September, 1972, quite certain that it would not be approved, but realizing that this was a necessary strategic step toward building interest in the issue. After their request was denied by a 5–2 vote, they launched a referendum drive. Petition signatures were obtained, for the most part, by standing outside the polls during the October primary election. Taking advantage of state laws concerning the scheduling of referenda, they timed their filing of the petition so that the city would be forced to put it on the general election ballot in November.

Once on the ballot, the question received very little attention. One of the two daily papers editorialized against districts, but the few news stories devoted to the referendum were short and obscure. Proponents spent no money on advertising; their expenditures totaled $56.00, used to print and copy their petitions. They did, however, mobilize a door-to-door campaign in the neighborhoods they represented. The Chamber of Commerce announced its opposition, as did the Raleigh Merchants Bureau, the mayor, and four of the other six council members. To these expected opponents were added the League of Women Voters, and the principal black political organization, the Raleigh Citizens Association (RCA). The only active public campaigning came at hearings sponsored by the Junior Chamber of Commerce, which were poorly attended.

In the black community, opinion was divided; although the RCA opposed the change, the black council member supported it. One problem was in the wording of the proposal: It stipulated five single-member districts and two at-large seats, but did not specify where district lines would be drawn. Blacks, numbering about one-fifth of the voters, could not be sure that their situation would be improved. Of apparent benefit to opponents was the city attorney's ruling that any district lines drawn at that time might have to be redrawn in line with registration figures at the time of the next election.

The district question was itself overshadowed by two other electoral events. It was to share the ballot with the 1972 presidential election, and with a referendum on consolidation of the city and county school systems. Opponents of consolidation linked such a merger to increased busing, and the resultant discussion was confused but attention-grabbing.

The district representation referendum was approved by 52 percent of those voting on it, and thus came into effect with the local elections of 1973. The total vote on districts represented only 51 percent of Raleigh's registered voters, just 70 percent of those who had voted for president on the same ballot. The level of voting on this issue in various types of precincts is shown in Table 2.4. From analysis of these aggregate data, it becomes clear that the referendum's success rested with its relatively high level of support in middle-income white precincts. Although it was sup-

Table 3.4. Raleigh: Referendum Turnout and Support
for District Representation, 1972

Precinct Type	Mean Vote on Districts as % of Vote for President	Mean Vote on Districts as % Registered Voters	Mean Vote in Favor of Districts
Over 50% Black (5)	32	19	54
White, Mean House (10) value over $25,000	77	59	44
White, Mean House (9) value between $15–25,000	76	52	58
White, Mean House (9) value less than $15,000	69	45	49

ported by a majority of those voting on the issue in the black precincts, less than one-third of black-precinct residents voting for president even voted on the district issue; this represented only 19 percent of voters registered in those precincts. In white precincts, the relationship between average house value and vote for districts was curvilinear, as reflected in the fact that in precincts with average house values less than $20,500, the correlation was +.48, whereas in precincts with values higher than that amount, the correlation was −.75 (for an overall correlation of −.35). Because of the inferred busing component in the school district merger vote, it took on an ideological tone. The vote in favor of merger showed an inverse correlation with the vote for George Wallace in the presidential primary that year of −.94. The district proposal, however, did not produce any such left-right split: The correlation between vote for districts and for George Wallace was −.11. This gives some support to the description of prodistrict forces as an amalgam of "conservative antibusers, liberal college professors, Wallace factory workers, and suburban technocrats" (Raleigh *News and Observer*, April 19, 1976). It is important to recall, however, that very little attention was given to the proposal in comparison with other issues on voters' minds, and that the black leadership was divided as to how it would affect minority political power. It was carried largely on the initiative of a few white neighborhood activists.

The mid-1970s were a period of peak influence for Raleigh's neighborhood representatives on the council. The black council member, Clarence Lightner, was elected Mayor in 1973. He was defeated by a "downtown" candidate in 1975, but the 1977 Mayor's race was won by the "little old lady in tennis shoes," Isabella Cannon. In recent years, however, the architects of the district system sense that they have lost control of the council, which has had a majority coalition from the affluent districts and the at-large seats, and has not been sympathetic to neighborhood-group concerns. Even so, there has been discussion of a referendum to return to the at-large system, an idea promoted by the director of the Raleigh Merchants' Bureau. However, the controversy that earlier characterized the system of representation seems largely to have subsided. Blacks, as we shall see, have been largely unaffected by districts, and continue to be bystanders on the district issue.

Sacramento. Sacramento has a minority population roughly proportionate to that in the North Carolina cities (see Table 2.3); that population is, however, divided among black, Asian, and Spanish-speaking populations. As a consequence, the dispersion of minority residential areas is much greater in Sacramento than in Charlotte or Raleigh.

Browning, Marshall, and Tabb (1979: 6) describe the movement to district representation in Sacramento as one product of a liberal Democratic challenge to a conservative, generally Republican coalition in control of local government. The challengers referred to those in control as "South Tammany Park," as most of them lived in an upper-income neighborhood known as South Land Park. The new liberal coalition had ties to both black and Hispanic groups, and had elected two minority members to the at-large council before the shift to an all-district system in 1971. They created a prodistrict organization to propose the district charter amendment in 1969, and organized for that purpose as Sacramentans for Charter Amendments Now (SCAN). They were opposed by a group for the "old guard" known as the Sacramento Committee Against Reform Elections (SCARE) (*Sacramento Bee*, June 21, 1969).

SCAN went before the council to propose the appointment of a citizens' committee to review the charter. The council complied, appointing a committee with members from business, labor, minorities, neighborhoods, the League of Women Voters, and the Democratic and Republican parties. This committee drew up a charter amendment which, after considerable discussion, the council agreed to put on the ballot.

The district campaign appeared to draw little public interest. Editorials for the reform appeared in the *Sacramento Bee*, while the *Sacramento Union* came out in opposition. The eight weeks between the council decision placing the issue on the ballot and the election date foreclosed any possibility of extensive organizational efforts. Only 29 percent of the electorate voted on June 24, 1969, and the measure was defeated by a 3–2 margin.

There was no clear involvement by minority leaders in the 1969 referendum. A white representative of SCAN was quoted by the *Bee* to the effect that "minorities don't feel that they have a voice on the City Council. . . . Many of the areas of the city where they are concentrated as far as housing goes are not represented on the council. It is our hope that the district system will provide for those areas the opportunity to elect their own representatives . . . . This would give their vote a lot more meaning." Apparently minorities did not lack surrogate representation on the issue, but there is no indication of intensity of feeling on their part.

The liberal coalition revived the issue in 1970, with greater grassroots organization, door-to-door campaigning, and public meetings. This time, with the measure on the general election ballot, and with no apparent organized opposition, an eight-district system was approved by a margin of 57 to 43 percent, with a turnout of 78 percent.

Districts have been in place in Sacramento since 1971, and the system has not become an issue since that time, even though it provides for no at-large representation other than the mayor. It is important to note the effect of Sacramento's minority dispersion: Blacks, Chicanos, and Asians combined do not constitute a majority of the voters in any district. It is hardly surprising that the district system is not a focus of polarization in Sacramento.

The political dynamics by which the district system was adopted in Charlotte, Raleigh and Sacramento were quite similar. Differences in effects can be predicted rather well from variation in the ethnic composition and population distribution in each city.

Ahead of Their Time: Earlier Cases of Change

Although we have identified the decade of the seventies as the high point of a trend toward district representation, we have also studied three cities where change in the structure of representation took place in the 1960s. These cities were included to provide cases with a longer period of time under districts, and, thus, greater reliability in assessing effects of the change. Descriptions of the political dynamics leading to change in Des Moines, Peoria, and Memphis can be useful also, however, in showing the process of change to districts in the absence of federal interest or involvement, and, in the first two cases, in the absence of racial conflict as a factor. (As noted earlier, Peoria is our deviant case, its last change having been toward a more at-large plan.)

Des Moines. Des Moines's change in 1967 from a five-member at-large council to a mixed system with four district and two at-large members was a secondary consequence of that city's long conflict over the city manager form of government. In 1907, Des Moines became the second city in the United States to adopt the commission system, the original choice of progressive reformers. By the 1940s, however, that government was pictured by latter day Des Moines reformers as inefficient, corrupt and under the influence of "special interests"; in 1945, a city manager system was established by referendum. That change was supported in the largely white collar areas west of the Des Moines River, but opposed by blue-collar east siders. This class and geographical conflict over manager government continued through the 1950s and into the 1960s, as referenda on proposals to abolish the manager form were defeated in 1959 and 1963.

Opponents of manager government consistently cited three reasons for their position. First, they blamed high property taxes on manager government. Second, they claimed that the city was being dominated by "outsiders"; indeed, at the time of the 1959 referendum, the city manager, the planning director, the public works director, and the chief traffic engineer had been hired from outside Des Moines. Finally, linking manager government and at-large elections, opponents argued that east siders were rarely elected to council, a claim we will document in the following chapter.

In addition, the most active opponents of manager government held and articulated strongly conservative beliefs which contrasted with the somewhat progressive views of the "establishment". This was not by any means a battle between conservatives and ideological liberals, but in the context of the late fifties and early sixties, it was an emotional clash between two distinctive groups of people with clearly differing world views.

Despite victories by promanager forces, opponents remained vocal and active. In 1967, two petitions regarding changes in city structure were circulated. East siders advocated replacing the manager/at-large system with a mayor/district council system. The League of Women Voters, strong supporters of manager government since the 1940s, simply proposed a change to a mixed council. After the east sider's petition was ruled illegal on a technicality,[9] they gave their support to the League proposal. While both groups worked for adoption of a mixed council, there was no communication or cooperation between them during the campaign; they did not, in reality, want the same things from the new system of government. In comparison with the heated campaigns of 1959 and 1963, the 1967 proposal carried with 54 percent of the vote in a rather lackluster election; the proposal gained 71 percent of the vote on the east side but only 41 percent of the west side vote.

What occurred, it appears, was an exchange. East side opponents of manager government, unable to win seats on the old council, agreed at least temporarily to drop that opposition in return for gaining east side council seats. Manager supporters saved what was most important to them, but gave up the "establishment" or west-side monopoly of council seats.

After fifteen years in operation, the mixed council seems an accepted part of Des Moines government. In addition, current east side council members articulate "us-versus-them" attitudes less frequently than many of the original east-side activists. This does not mean, however, that the conflict has completely disappeared. In the fall of 1979, a proposal to elect four of seven school board members by wards was defeated by a margin of 58 to 42 percent; most of the precincts where the plan carried were on the east side, while most of the precincts where it was defeated were on the west side.

Memphis. There is perhaps no more telling example of the failure of the commission form of government to live up to the hopes the reformers placed in it than in the fact that Mayor Ed Crump introduced the commission to Memphis in 1910, and proceeded to use it as the basis for an archetypal political machine. From 1909 until his death in 1954, Crump ran the Memphis machine through a coalition of white ethnics, blacks, businessmen, and persons involved in gambling, saloons, and prostitution. However, since foreign-born persons made up only 5 percent of the Memphis citizenry, the 40 percent of the population that was black was crucial to Crump's political control. (Tucker, 1980: 17)

Crump died in 1954. Without his guiding hand, Memphis government in the late 1950s and early 1960s was in great disarray. In the aftermath of the machine's demise, various groups and movements struggled for local political influence, either by attempting to capture a majority on the existing commission, or by reforming it to their advantage. One reform drive was launched in 1962 to both merge the city and county governments and eliminate the commission form, but in the ensuing referendum the voters rejected the proposal. (Tucker, 106–110)

In 1963, William B. Ingram Jr. was elected mayor in a populist-style campaign that attracted support from black, working-class, and middle-class conservatives who feared a property tax increase. The city's business leaders were somewhat alarmed that for the first time a mayor had been elected without their support. Their reaction is tellingly summed up in a letter from Lucius Burch, a prominent attorney, to Fred Ahlgren, editor of the Memphis *Commercial Appeal*:

> The situation existing in the City Commission is going to result in four years of anarchy unless Ingram is able to obtain control of the Commissioners. Either will be bad. I have known Ingram for many years. . . . He is intelligent and has an intuitive awareness of what pleases the masses. But what I am concerned with is not Judge Ingram and I mention this only to justify the prophesy of parlous times ahead.
>
> What is now highlighted are the inherent weaknesses and insufficiencies of our form of municipal government. Some good can be made to come out of the chaos if the example spurs the electorate to reform the city charter, which is now easily possible under the home rule amendment to the Constitution.
>
> What I am proposing for your consideration and support is the formation of a truly representative body of citizens to undertake a serious study of our charter and the various forms of city government with the purpose of finally arriving at a consensus as to the best form of government for this city and then

supplying the political leadership and effort to institute the form of government agreed upon as desirable.

. . . .Those participating as members of the study committee would have to be truly representative of the power structure of the city. This would insure that all partisan viewpoints were accommodated in the study and there would then be a sufficiently broad base for political activity to accomplish the desired result. To select the right membership of the committee is not as simple as it sounds because events of the recent past has shown that what we generally believe to be the power structure of the city is not now in many cases politically effective. The results of the election respecting consolidation and Ingram's election are examples that come to mind.[10]

Burch and Ahlgren called a meeting of 277 local leaders to elect a "Program of Progress" committee to propose a new city charter. Positions held by members of this committee were not in line with their national political allegiances. Memphis had been undergoing a dramatic party realignment with the emergence of the civil rights movement in the early 1960s. As blacks deserted the Republican Party, whites moved toward the GOP, supporting both Goldwater and the Republican congressional candidate in 1964 by margins of two-to-one. On the Program of Progress committee, blacks and Republicans both supported a district system; each of these groups assumed districts would enhance their representation. (Republicans also supported a run-off election provision, which would avoid the election of blacks by a plurality in districts where a majority of voters were white.) Chamber of Commerce leaders, on the other hand, generally favored an at-large system, and the committee finally agreed to a compromise charter proposal including a council of seven districts and six at-large seats, in addition to a strong mayor. The mixed council would assure white control, while, for the first time, blacks would be guaranteed some council seats.

The only opposition to the change coalesced around Mayor Ingram, but much of his earlier base of support had been brought into the new reform coalition. The mixed district/at-large system was adopted by a 60–40 margin, and the first city council election was scheduled for 1967.

As predicted, the first council included three blacks. Republicans made more dramatic gains, however, for there were no Democrats among the ten white members, only Republicans and independents. At a time of change in party identification, the elimination of established offices and their incumbents accelerated the political harvest for the Republican Party. In the long run, however, the new Republican preeminence made districts less useful to them—they were no longer a minority group, and would also probably have gained control under the commission system eventually. The mayor's office was captured by a staunchly conservative segregationist in a racially polarized vote that foreshadowed the predominance of racial problems on Memphis's political agenda through the 1970s.

Although there has been no discussion of further change in the system of council representation in Memphis, this cannot be interpreted as a sign of general satisfaction with the council. Both blacks and whites express the view that the council has been ineffective in dealing with Memphis's overriding racial split. Blacks found that their minority representation gave them no leverage on the dramatic issues of school integration and the sanitation workers' strike that occasioned the assassination of Martin Luther King. When recalcitrance in responding to black demands was highlighted by that tragic event, the negative national image that resulted stirred the business elite into action. It was the Chamber of Commerce, not city government, that took the initiative to bring blacks more into the mainstream of Memphis's economic and social life. It is now commonly perceived that neither black nor white council members are community leaders, and the council's role in the community is no larger than its limited formal powers.

The Memphis case is unique in that it illustrates the adoption of district representation without a federal presence or involvement, but involving the issue of minority representation. In this case, social and economic change led business elites to favor centralization of political authority in order to achieve more efficiently the goals they set for the city, including a more modern image. Blacks supported them in order finally to enter the decision-making process. In the aftermath, there was no euphoria in either group, as one might expect from a political change engineered with so little conflict. If the battle was won so easily, could anything of significance have been gained?

Peoria. Peoria has changed governmental structure, including type of council representation, three times since 1951. During the 1970s, it was a deviant case, adding at-large representation at a time when no other large city was moving in that direction.

In 1951, a partisan mayor/district council system was replaced by a non-partisan manager/at-large council government. This system resulted from a classic "reform" campaign against corruption and inefficiency. (Martin, 1974). However, politicians of both parties with strong followings in Peoria's then-populous working class areas led a successful drive for readoption of a partisan, district council; this change was made by referendum in 1960.

Politics and government in Peoria became particularly chaotic and conflictual following the election of a new mayor and council in 1969. The ten-district council included five members elected with the grass roots support of a conservatively oriented group which had organized to fight the imposition of a utility tax. These five members often voted in a bloc. The other councilmen were not as closely allied, but actions by their colleagues often seemed to create a second bloc and, in specific situations, one of the more progressive members worked at coalition-building. In addition, the new mayor, a neophyte to public office troubled with personal problems, never gained control of council meetings; heated arguments, personal insults and other unseemly exchanges became standard fare during council proceedings.

The League of Women Voters took advantage of the council's problems to argue once more for at-large representation. In 1972, the League organized a successful referendum campaign which resulted in adoption of the current mixed system of five district and three at-large representatives.

As in Des Moines, the concept of a mixed system has gained widespread acceptance. However, white political activists from working class areas argue that current district lines limit them to one representative, while black groups argue that these lines have kept them from gaining any representation. Conflicts over representation in Peoria in the near future, at least, will probably center on redrawing boundaries for the five current districts rather than on the overall structure of council elections.

This discussion of details from individual case studies may tire the reader impatient for general conclusions. A careful reading, however, validates our strategy of combining the contextual richness of case studies with a common framework of statistical analysis. It is certainly appropriate to summarize these eleven cities in terms of local initiative or federal intervention, but the case-by-case descriptions point rather to a continuum of greater or lesser outside involvement, from the formally court-ordered change, through preemptive local action, to situations where a federal role was never envisaged. One can identify patterns of alliances among various groups, but the cases present a rich mosaic of possibilities of coalition among business leaders, minority groups, neighborhood organizations and others, conditioned by the nature of the preexisting system, the relative size of minority populations, the challenges and constraints of economic modernization, and the interplay between political trends at the local and national level. These descriptions must give pause to anyone who would presume that given forms of representation invariably work to the advantage of given social and economic groups. While keeping in mind these idiosyncratic factors that otherwise could distort conclusions based on a modest-sized sample, our analysis will now return to a more rigorous framework of comparison.

NOTES

1   The following discussion draws largely on O'Rourke, 1979.

2   In practice, most jurisdictions seek clearance through the Justice Department, since this is seen as the less time-consuming and less expensive route.

3   This discussion is largely based on Cotrell and Stevens, 1978: 79–87, and Cotrell and Fleischmann, 1979.

4   The following discussion relies heavily on O'Rourke, 197.

5   437 U.S. 535, at 550 (Rehnquist, J., concurring), as reported in O'Rourke, 1979: 26.

6   We are indebted to Arnold Fleischman for a first draft of this section on Fort Worth.

7   The precinct-level correlation of approval rates of the arts center and the science museum was over .99; thus the arts center vote will be used as a single indicator of the bond referendum vote.

8   See, for example, Hadden, Masotti and Thiessen (1968), Pilat (1968), and Cuomo (1974).

9   The city attorney ruled that the petition of the east siders violated state law governing the modification of municipal electoral structure.

10   Quoted in Tucker, 1980, pp. 112–113.

4

The Politics of District Elections

W E TURN NOW to our major task, determining what changes in local politics and government accompanied shifts from at-large to district representation.

According to criticisms of at-large elections, the advantage they give to affluent groups renders other citizens apathetic, and the less affluent do not run for at-large seats. The modification of electoral structure described in previous chapters provides an opportunity to test and compare the effect of these changes on recruitment and turnout. Do greater proportions of minorities and persons of low economic status run for and get elected to district councils? What change is observed in the financing of campaigns? Does turnout increase? Particularly, does it increase in previously underrepresented areas?

THE RECRUITMENT AND ELECTION OF COUNCIL MEMBERS

It is a commonplace that the theory of democracy is most difficult to put into practice in leadership recruitment. Robert Dahl observes that, although a variety of resources are available in the political arena, these resources tend to be cumulative in distribution (1963: 15). To counteract

57

this tendency, district proponents have sought to widen access to leader-ship roles by creating constituencies in which community-level minorities will be majorities, and by reducing the costs of campaigning. Adoption of district systems obviously results in geographic dispersion among council candidates and members, although this effect may be reduced in mixed systems. But what impact does this forced dispersion have on the homogeneity of councils along racial, class, and economic dimensions? We have hypothesized that:

1. Racial and residential diversity will increase.
2. More persons of white-collar and blue-collar status will run for council seats.
3. More persons of white-collar and blue-collar status will win council seats.

RACE AND DISTRICTS

The effect of districts on the racial composition of candidate pools has already been examined for blacks by Karnig and Welch (1980: 85–87). Using a data base of the 264 cities over 25,000 and at least 10 percent black, they found a greater number of black candidates per council seat in districted than in at-large cities. Our analysis has, once again, the vir-tue of controlling for many extraneous variables by focusing on the same cities with and without districts. Table 4.1 shows solid support of the Karnig-Welch thesis, for in each of the eleven cities districting led to greater proportions of minority candidates.

Does a greater number of candidates translate into a higher propor-tion of successful candidates? Karnig and Welch (1980: 70) found a strong positive relationship between proportions of black candidates and black council members. However, a reading of Table 4.2 will show that in our sample success depends upon the proportion of blacks in a city. Des Moines has scarcely any minority population to represent; but Peoria at 12 percent black had no minority representation under any system, and Raleigh and Sacramento at 23 and 24 percent minority population also show no noticeable change in minority representation. In Raleigh, successive black members held one of the seven at-large seats. The five districts established in 1972 included only one that was solidly black. Although there are still three at-large seats, only two blacks have run for them since 1972; prospective black candidates generally have chosen to contest among themselves for the "safe" seat, rather than at-tempt a city-wide race. Since neither of those who did run at-large came

Table 4.1. Candidates: Percentage of Total by Race

City	At-Large					District				
	White	Black	S/S	SS	Asian	White	Black	S/S	SS	Asian
San Antonio	68.4 (320)	4.3 (20)	27.4 (128)			48.5 (49)	10.9 (11)	40.6 (41)		
Richmond	78.3 (47)	21.7 (13)	—			65.1 (56)	34.9 (30)	—		
Charlotte	93.3 (320)	6.7 (23)	—			83.3 (60)	16.7 (12)	—		
Dallas	89.6 (259)	7.6 (22)	2.8 (8)			65.9 (56)	27.1 (23)	7.1 (6)		
Fort Worth	94.1 (285)	4.0 (12)	2.0 (6)			63.5 (33)	25.0 (13)	11.5 (6)		
Memphis	98.0 (49)	2.0 (1)	—			75.6 (205)	24.4 (66)	—		
Montgomery	94.9 (37)	5.1 (2)	—			67.9 (76)	32.1 (36)	—		
Des Moines	100.0 (—)	—	—			100.0 (—)	—	—		
Peoria	89.9 (89)	10.1 (9)	—			93.5 (158)	6.5 (11)	—		
Raleigh	91.2 (52)	8.8 (5)	—			82.6 (71)	17.4 (15)	—		
Sacramento	85.7 (66)	5.2 (4)		2.6 (2)	6.5 (5)	82.2 (111)	1.5 (2)		12.6 (17)	3.7 (5)

Table 4.2. Composition of Councils by Race

City	Before				After			
	White	Black	S/S	Asian	White	Black	S/S	Asian
Richmond	80.0 (20)	20.0 (5)	—	—	48.1 (13)	51.9 (14)	—	—
San Antonio	70.7 (82)	5.2 (6)	24.1 (28)	—	45.0 (9)	10.0 (2)	45.0 (9)	—
Charlotte	93.6 (103)	6.4 (7)	—	—	81.0 (17)	19.0 (4)	—	—
Dallas	93.9 (107)	3.5 (4)	2.6 (3)	—	78.8 (26)	18.2 (6)	3.0 (1)	—
Fort Worth	95.5 (111)	4.5 (5)	0 (0)	—	62.5 (10)	25.0 (4)	12.5 (2)	—
Memphis	93.8 (15)	6.2 (1)	—	—	78.9 (45)	21.1 (12)	—	—
Montgomery	94.9 (37)	5.1 (2)	—	—	63.3 (13)	36.7 (8)	—	—
Sacramento	77.8 (21)	7.4 (2)	3.7 (1)	11.1 (3)	80.0 (16)	10.0 (2)	5.0 (1)	5.0 (1)
Raleigh	85.7 (18)	14.3 (3)	—	—	85.2 (23)	14.8 (4)	—	—
Peoria	100.0	—	—	—	100.0	—	—	—
Des Moines	100.0	—	—	—	100.0	—	—	—

close to being elected, fighting over the black district may be the prudent approach.

In Sacramento, the 15 percent black and 9 percent Spanish-speaking population do not constitute a majority in any of the eight districts, either separately or combined. Thus, their voting strength is not appreciably enhanced. Our study suggests that a minority population must comprise about 30 percent of the total and be geographically concentrated for a district plan to result in increased representation, although this will of course depend on the number of districts. Our general survey of U.S. cities, referred to in Chapter 1, supplements the eleven-city study, more definitively to measure the impact of the change to districts on minority representation. It provides data on the equity of minority representation before and after change to districts, as well as on the circumstances of that change. These data cover the years between 1970 and the present for all cities, as well as the 1960s for cities outside the South. Data for the 1960s were not included for southern cities, since black enfranchisement during that decade might have uncontrollable effects on the findings.

For this larger data set we employed the Karnig measure of representational equity described in Chapter 1 (calculated by dividing the percentage of blacks on council by the percentage of blacks in the population). We have determined a current (1980-1) value, an average value for the 1970s or for the years in the decade before the change to districts, and, for northern cities, an average equity value for the 1960s. These scores, along with the difference between current scores and the 1970s average for all cities, are shown in Table 4.3. In addition, differences between

Table 4.3. **Regional Difference in Average Equity Scores and Changes in Average Equity Scores**

	North	South
Current	.76	.51
(N)	(101)	(193)
1970s Average	.60	.29
	(85)	(185)
1960s Average	.34	—
	(104)	
Difference, Current—1970s	.15	.21
	(85)	(185)
Difference, 1970s—1960s	.23	—
	(83)	
Difference, 1980—1960s	.39	—
	(87)	

current scores/1960s average and 1970s/1960s are shown for non-southern cities.

As Table 4.3 indicates, current black equity scores are higher outside the South; equity levels in northern cities also averaged considerably higher during the 1970s. However, the magnitude of that difference has narrowed as southern equity scores gained an average of .21 during the past decade compared to a .15 increase in equity levels for cities outside the South. How important is the impact of change in the electoral structure in explaining this trend? Table 4.4 shows that, although southern cities which already had district or mixed councils in 1970 had higher equity scores than those with at-large councils during the 1970s, all southern scores were considerably lower than those found in cities with similar electoral systems outside the South.

There was a .28 regional difference (.53 to .25) in equity scores between northern and southern at-large cities, a .19 difference for mixed system cities, and a .18 difference between district cities.

Current scores show a different pattern. While the margin between at-large cities has remained almost constant at .30 (.67 to .37), the difference between mixed systems has dropped to .08 (.76 to .68), while the gap between district cities has narrowed to .09 (.96 to .87). It should also be noted, of course, that equity scores in northern district cities are very close to a value of one, indicating that blacks in these cities have council representation that is nearly proportional to their portion of the population. If blacks in the South are to gain similar equity, it will undoubtedly be in cities with district elections. Table 4.5 shows that strikingly different changes in equity occurred during the 1970s in southern cities, depending upon electoral backgrounds. At-large cities increased only

Table 4.4. Equity Scores by Region and Governmental Structure

Structure	Current		1970s		Difference Current—1970s	
	North	South	North	South*	North	South[6]
At-Large	.67	.37	.53	.25	.16	.06
	(53)	122)	(51)	(164)	(51)	(117)
Mixed	.76	.68	.66	.45	.12	.43
	(16)	(30)	(15)	(10)	(15)	(30)
District	.96	.87	.71	.53	.13	.54
	(22)	(43)	(19)	(15)	(19)	(43)

*Prechange data from cities which changed from at-large to district or mixed systems are included in the at-large category.

†Prechange data from cities which changed structure were included in their *new* form of government in calculating changes in equity.

Table 4.5. Southern City Equity Scores
by Former and Present Electoral Structure

Structure	Current	1970s	Difference Current—1970s
At-Large			
No District efforts	.39	.34	.05
(N)	(85)	(82)	(82)
Unsuccessful District Efforts	.33	.24	.09
	(37)	(35)	(35)
Mixed			
Before 1970	.57	.45	.13
	(10)	(10)	(10)
Changed During 1970s	.70	.11	.61
	(20)	(20)	(20)
District			
Before 1970	.85	.53	.33
	(16)	(15)	(15)
Changed During 1970s	.89	.10	.73
	(28)	(28)	(28)

.06, cities with mixed systems in place in 1970 increased .13, and cities which elected by district in 1970 increased equity scores by 33 points. Enormous increases are found in the cities which adopted new electoral systems; cities which changed from at-large to mixed systems show a .61 increase in equity, while those which adopted district systems had an even greater increase of .73.

From our intensive study of eleven cities, we were able to identify factors that might mitigate or even nullify the effects of districting on minority representation in particular cases, as in that of Raleigh. However, the evidence overall supports our first hypothesis: Minority citizens have achieved greater equity in local representation as a result of the movement to districts.

STATUS AND DISTRICTS

We have hypothesized that districts will result in increased candidacies and increased electoral victories by persons of white- and blue-collar status. Like beauty, the desirable qualities of a council member lie largely in the eye of the beholder. The classic reformist thinking held that the best system was one that brought the better class of citizen into public office. This view is often expressed in contemporary circles when a system is deplored because "you simply can't get a good businessman to run for office." On the other hand, the Jacksonian belief that any citizen is or should be capable of fulfilling the duties of public office leads to a finding of virtue in changes that bring more diversity of occupation and background into the political arena.

However wide the difference in these preferences, they are based on a common assumption that—for better or worse—district systems result in more diverse and generally lower-status councils. Such an assumption may appear to be a truism, but at times the obvious does not stand up to empirical testing.

The district system at least guarantees a certain amount of diversity in location of residence. Table 4.6 shows the distribution of council representation among districts as classified by racial composition and average house value. It generally shows the greater representation of minorities under districts, and less consistently of lower- and middle-income whites. Since it does not reflect the *proportion* of districts in each category, however, the equity of representation is not evident. Table 4.7 corrects for this by showing the proportion of representatives, district or at-large, living in each category of district, divided by the proportion of districts in that category. If we can assume that districts have roughly equal population, then true equity is achieved under the pure district system, and the degree of departure from that standard is seen in the equity scores of mixed and at-large systems. Upper- and middle-income white neighborhoods have been disproportionately represented in the at-large systems of all cities under study here. The change in equity with districts is thus particularly striking in the cities tha moved from all-at-large to all-district councils, especially for minorities.

It is not necessarily the case, however, that poor or lower-status neighborhoods will be represented by individuals typical of their populations. Thus, the diversity of council membership was further tested by categorizing council candidates—and separately, successful candidates—according to standard census-based definitions of their occupations. Our findings are based on the following groups: (1) professional, (2) business people, (3) clerical and sales personnel, (4) blue-collar workers and (5) other, including students and housewives.

Business people have dominated most of the predistrict elections (see Table 4.8), composing absolute majorities of the candidates in four of our cities, and over 40 percent of them in two others.

Table 4.6. Geographic Distribution of Council Members by District Type

		Black/ Spanish		White Lower-Income*		Middle-Income*		Upper-Income	
		%	N	%	N	%	N	%	N
(cities now all-district)									
Richmond	pre-D	33	(9)	—		19	(5)	48	(13)
	post-D	44	(12)	—		44	(12)	11	(3)
San Antonio	pre-D	37	(25)	10	(7)	22	(15)	31	(21)
	post-D	60	(6)	10	(1)	10	(1)	20	(2)
Fort Worth	pre-D	8	(5)	20	(13)	18	(12)	54	(35)
	post-D	25	(4)	25	(4)	37.5	(6)	12.5	(2)
Montgomery	pre-D	0		0		11	(1)	89	(8)
	pre-D	37.5	(3)	12.5	(1)	12.5	(1)	50	(4)
Sacramento	pre-D	—		7	(2)	59	(16)	33	(9)
	post-D	—		37.5	(9)	37.5	(9)	25	(16)
(cities now under mixed at-large/district systems)									
		%	N	%	N	%	N	%	N
Charlotte	pre-D	15	(8)	—		30	(16)	55	(29)
	post-D	32	(7)	—		23	(5)	45	(10)
Dallas	pre-D	7	(5)	13	(9)	24	(16)	56	(38)
	post-D	19	(6)	10	(3)	19	(6)	52	(16)
Memphis	pre-D	0		0		63	(13)	38	(8)
	post-D	24	(10)	0		29	(12)	48	(20)
Raleigh	pre-D	14	(3)	—		0		86	(18)
	post-D	15	(4)	—		30	(8)	56	(15)
Des Moines	pre-D	—		7	(2)	70	(21)	23	(7)
	post-D	—		21	(7)	47	(16)	32	(11)
Peoria	present	—		17	(4)	26	(6)	57	(13)
	Dist.Sys.	—		17	(3)	39	(7)	44	(8)

*As in Chapter 2 (see Tables 2.3 and 2.4) average income is measured through the surrogate of house value, since this is the only income-related measure available by census bloc. We have consistently classified the eighty districts in these eleven cities as lower-, middle-, or upper-income, defined by average house values in the precincts making up the district. If that average was less than $14,000 according to the 1970 census, the district is classified as lower-income. Middle income comprises the range from $14,001 to $20,000, with upper income consisting of those averaging over $20,000.

Table 4.7. **Representational Equity According to Current Districts**

Type of District by Racial and Income Characteristics

City		Black/ Spanish	White Lower- Income	Middle- Income	Upper- Income
		(Pre-District Scores for Cities Now all-District)			
Richmond		.75	—	.43	4.36
San Antonio		.62	1.00	2.20	1.55
Fort Worth		.32	.80	.48	4.32
Montgomery		0.00	0.00	1.0	2.02
Sacramento		—	.19	1.57	1.32
	Cities Now Under Mixed, At-Large/District Systems				
Charlotte	pre-D	.35	—	1.03	1.90
	post-D	.74	—	.79	1.55
Dallas	pre-D	.28	1.04	.96	1.49
	post-D	.76	.80	.76	1.39
Memphis	pre-D	0.00	0.00	1.65	1.52
	post-D	.64	—	.77	1.92
Raleigh	pre-D	.70	—	0.00	2.15
	post-D	.75	—	.75	1.4
Des Moines	pre-D	—	.28	1.4	.92
	post-D	—	.84	.94	1.28
Peoria	present	—	.85	.65	1.42
	dist.syst.	—	.85	.97	1.10

For this purpose, representatives in the predistrict systems are classified as to their district of residence at the time of adoption of districts. The equity score here is the proportion of seats from districts of a given income or ethnic classification, divided by the proportion of districts in that classification (assuming that districts are of equal population in each city). Equity scores for all categories in an all-district system are by this definition equal to 1.0.

After the change to districts, the proportion of business candidates drops dramatically in every city but Memphis and Montgomery; the exceptions are the cities that also changed from a commission to a mayor-council form, and the fact that they are contrary to the trend may be tied to this structural difference. One must interpret this change in occupational background cautiously, for modernization and the increasing importance of local government decision making in the 1960s may also have contributed to the waning presence and influence of small business owners. The abruptness of the change at the time of structural reform, however, suggests that districts at least cleared the way for large numbers

Table 4.8. Occupational Composition of Candidate Pools

City	% Professional		% Business		% Clerical/Sales Blue Collar		% Other (Students, Housewives)	
	Before	After	Before	After	Before	After	Before	After
Richmond	32.8 (19)	39.0 (32)	41.4 (24)	36.6 (30)	22.4 (13)	23.2 (19)	3.4 (2)	1.2 (1)
San Antonio	33.4 (131)	36.8 (32)	28.6 (112)	12.6 (11)	28.1 (110)	37.9 (33)	9.9 (39)	12.6 (11)
Charlotte	18.3 (60)	41.4 (29)	53.8 (176)	30.0 (21)	25.7 (84)	28.6 (20)	2.1 (7)	0.0 (0)
Dallas	31.7 (86)	42.7 (32)	57.2 (155)	38.7 (29)	7.3 (20)	16.0 (12)	3.7 (10)	2.7 (2)
Fort Worth	26.4 (73)	32.0 (16)	63.2 (175)	52.0 (26)	9.0 (25)	12.0 (6)	1.4 (4)	4.0 (2)
Memphis	50.0 (23)	43.5 (117)	26.1 (12)	27.9 (75)	23.9 (11)	27.2 (73)	0.0 (0)	1.5 (4)
Montgomery	47.4 (18)	27.0 (38)	34.2 (13)	36.2 (51)	15.8 (6)	29.8 (42)	2.6 (1)	7.1 (10)
Sacramento	49.3 (69)	85.5 (65)	28.6 (40)	2.6 (2)	17.9 (25)	5.2 (4)	4.2 (6)	6.6 (5)
Raleigh	29.1 (16)	54.9 (45)	63.6 (35)	29.3 (24)	5.5 (3)	13.4 (11)	1.8 (1)	2.4 (2)
Des Moines	29.4 (30)	25.9 (30)	45.1 (46)	37.1 (43)	23.5 (24)	30.2 (35)	2.0 (2)	6.9 (8)
Peoria	32.6 (31) 36.7 (55)	41.4 (30)	31.6 (30) 30.0 (45)	35.6 (26)	32.6 (31) 32.7 (49)	21.9 (16)	3.2 (3) 0.7 (1)	1.4 (1)

of nonincumbent candidacies to reflect the increased political involvement of professionals.

In every case but Des Moines, the proportion of professionals increases as the proportion of business representative shrinks. However, there is also a striking democratization of the candidate pool under districts, evidenced in the uniformly higher proportion of white and blue-collar employees who run for council. This is seen in another form in Des Moines and Peoria, where blue-collar neighborhoods produce a greater share of the candidates under districts.

In order to assess the impact of structural change in representation on the social status of candidates and council members with more precision, an index rating the social desirability of one's occupation was applied to each case. This index was developed by the National Opinion Research Center (NORC), and is derived from survey research on general-public evaluations of occupations.[1] These evaluations are aggregated, and assigned a score on a range of 0 to 100. Actual scores vary from the 90s (architects, dentists, chemical engineers, lawyers and judges, and physicians and surgeons) to less than 5 (coal-mine laborers, thread and fabric mill operatives, porters, and saw and planing mill workers). We assume that the degree to which the mean of such scores approaches 100 is a relative measure of the elitist membership of a council. If popular assumptions and our predictions about the effects of districts are correct, then a change from at-large to district elections should result in (1) a drop in the mean status ranking of council members; and (2) an increase in the *dispersion* of these rankings, statistically expressed in the standard deviation.

Figure 4.1 allows for plotting each city on an X and Y axis according to the degree of change in status rankings at the time of districts. Points on the horizontal axis show the number of units of increase in the mean of members' NORC scores; points on the verticle axis shows units of reduction in the standard deviation as one moves toward the top of the page. Thus, if districts brought lower average status and greater diversity among candidates for council, the points should be in the lower left quadrant. If a council became higher status and more uniform, the city will be in the upper right quadrant. The actual plotting of change shows most (six) cities to be in the lower left, as predicted, but often by very few points. Three cities show an increase in means *and* standard deviations, and San Antonio shows a decrease in each. The second Peoria structural change resulted in higher status scores and less diversity, which accords with the hypothesis. Only Fort Worth is completely contrary to the prediction, especially in having less diversity with districts.

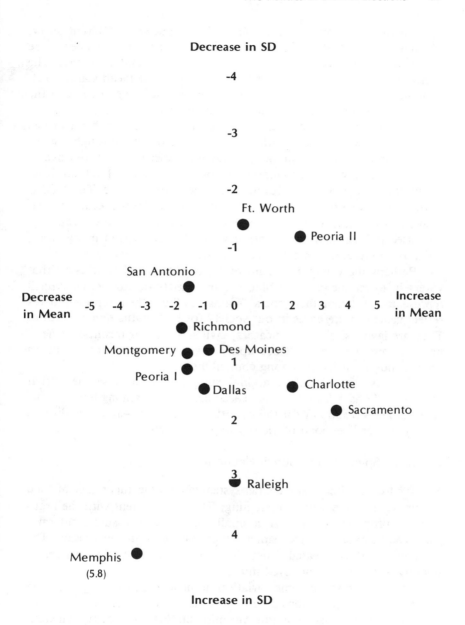

Figure 4.1. All Candidates: Change in Mean and Standard Deviation of NORC Occupational Status Ratings, Before/After Districts

On the other hand, Figure 4.2 tells a somewhat different story. When we look only at election winners—that is, at council members—the change to districts seems to have had an even more random impact. The overall tendency has been toward an *increase* in the mean status level, although in the majority of cities there has also been the increase in the standard deviation that we would have predicted.

To understand these findings, we must mention a problem in this type of time series research. All these cities are passing through a common historical period, although the changes described occurred over a span of nineteen years. A common phenomenon since the 1960s has been the increased interest of professional people in local office. The NORC status scale puts professionals at the top, with business executives, and then small business owners and operators further down in the ranking. Increased professional participation would be reflected in many cities, then, as an increase in mean social status.

Perhaps more important, however, is our overall conclusion that voters in lower income and blue collar districts do not select council representatives from their social status. Rather, their representatives reflect general preferences in our society for high status representation: They are lawyers, clergy, educators, civil servants, or business owners, not laborers or clerks. Geographic dispersion does not result in socioeconomic variation among council members.

We have found only marginal support for the hypothesis that district elections will result in increased candidacies among lower-status citizens, and no support for the hypothesis that lower-status candidates have a greater likelihood of victory under districts.

Campaign Spending in Council Elections

We hypothesized that a district system vitiates the importance of fund raising as an element of campaigning. This is consistent with the argument of proponents that with a small constituency, a successful campaign can be based on shoe leather rather than on media advertising. The candidate is thus released from the need either to be independently wealthy or to rely on moneyed interests.

Table 4.9 shows extreme variation in the level of campaign funding by city, from means of considerably less than $1,000 in the southeastern cities to several thousand in San Antonio and Sacramento. If high campaign costs are an evil to be remedied, this is a less salient problem in the East than in the West.

Interpreting the effects of funding on electoral success under any system is fraught with difficulty. A first problem is that most data on the

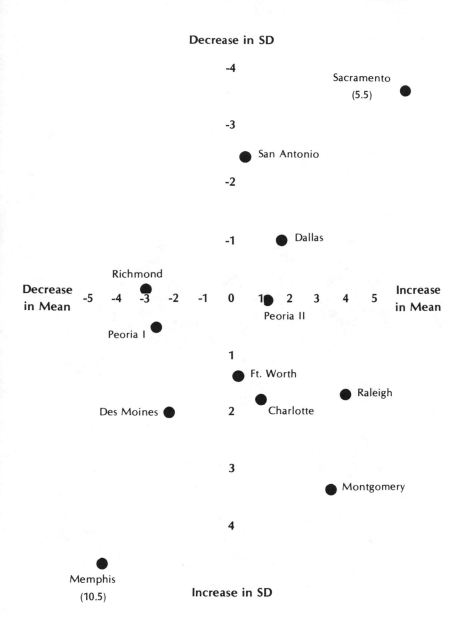

FIGURE 4.2. Council Members: Change in Mean and Standard Deviation of NORC Occupational Status Ratings, Before/After Districts

Table 4.9. Mean Campaign Expenditure in Council Elections*

City	All Candidates		Losers		Winners		District	At-Large
	Before	After	Before	After	Before	After	After	After
Charlotte	$ 329 (33)	$ 343 (72)	$ 172 (20)	$ 232 (50)	$ 710 (13)	$ 659 (19)	$ 252 (49)	$ 536 (23)
Richmond	—	146 (85)	—	139 (60)	—	173 (22)	146 (85)	—
San Antonio	6850 (113)	5033 (96)	3102 (89)	3195 (77)	19501 (24)	12482 (19)	5033 (96)	—
Dallas	615 (68)	1524 (81)	357 (46)	890 (48)	1180 (20)	2683 (26)	1289 (63)	2349 (18)
Fort Worth	286 (116)	592 (50)	131 (73)	409 (36)	605 (38)	1064 (14)	592 (50)	—
Memphis	—	938 (86)	—	725 (59)	—	1403 (27)	243 (43)	1633 (43)
Sacramento	3093 (78)	4077 (141)	1715 (51)	3991 (192)	5696 (27)	9059 (16)	4077 (141)	—
Raleigh	—	153 (74)	—	97 (49)	—	274 (24)	143 (44)	169 (30)

*Financial data were not available for Des Moines, Peoria, and Montgomery

subject are recent, dating only from the passage of Watergate-era reforms. Thus for many of our cities there is no prechange information. An additional problem in the comparison of successive time periods is the overall rapid inflation rate in campaign costs, with a result that any reduction of expenses in a district system may be hidden when the district system follows an at-large plan. Finally, it is nearly impossible to single out the effect of funding when in the real world it is confounded by incumbency, turnout levels, closeness of competition and other factors. In the mixed district/at-large systems of Charlotte, Dallas, Memphis, and Raleigh expenditures are uniformly higher for at-large than for district seats. (See Table 4.9). Beyond this, the data in Table 4.9 allow us to conclude only that winners generally spend more than losers (uncontested candidacies are excluded from this analysis).

Beyond these somewhat trivial findings, we can proceed only with a multivariate analysis that allows us to control statistically for the effect of factors other than campaign spending in attracting votes. This approach is also more precise in that it measures effects not just on winning or losing, but on the *proportion* of the votes awarded to each candidate.

Table 4.10 shows the standardized regression coefficients for a common set of factors before and after districting in the sample cities. These coefficients show the relative importance of each variable in predicting the proportion of the vote each candidate will receive in a given type of election in a given city. They have been standardized (given a mean of zero and a variance of one) so that variables with different types and distributions of measurement units can be compared. They have several limitations. (1) They measure straight-line relationships, and undervalue those that, for example, would be less true for lower- or upper- than for middle-income voters. (2) They are confounded by factors that are themselves highly interconnected, as when candidates who are white and who are incumbents attract campaign contributions for those very attributes. Thus, our discussions must be based only on differences of considerable magnitude in coefficients and usually only where the coefficients are derived from a large number of cases. Strictly speaking, the figures take on meaning only in comparison with coefficients for other factors in the same set of elections for the same city.

For those cases where data are available to calculate the effect on vote proportions of campaign dollars spent, the funding variable seems to add significantly to the prediction. Campaign spending is an especially powerful predictor in primary or first-ballot situations, as one might expect; by the time candidates have passed this first hurdle the range of spending and its relationship to success will have been considerably reduced. It is interesting that there appears to be no relationship between

Table 4.10. (Page 1) Standardized Regression Coefficients: Factors in Council Candidate Electoral Success

City and Election	Incumbency		Funds		NORC		SPAN		Black	
	Before	After	Before	After	Before	After	Before	After	Before	After
San Antonio										
Primary	.17	.09	.59*	.63*	.26*	.24	.10	.13	.01	-.01
General	-.26*	.33*	.54*	.28*	.10	.29*	.04	.16	-.03	.07
Richmond	.51*	.67*	—	.07	.28*	.13			.05	.25*
Charlotte										
Primary	.40*	.22	—	.30*	.35*	.40*			.01	.07
General	.45*	.50*	—	.10	.28*	.08			-.08	.26
Dallas										
Primary	.27	—	—	.68*	.10	-.08	—	.17	-.06	-.15
General	.59*	.41*	.09	.18*	-.01	.13	.01	-.09	-.08	-.07
Fort Worth										
Primary	.35*	.20	.48*	.64*	.10	.03	—	-.14	-.05	.10
General	.24*	.32	.32*	.28*	.03	.21	-.01	.06	-.02	.12
Memphis										
Primary	—	.42*	—	.35*	—	.12			**	-.21
General	.64*	.34*	—	.24*	.31*	.07				.23
Montgomery										
Primary	.69*	.56*			-.04	.15			-.03	-.14
General	.44	.45*			-.13	.32			**	.47
Raleigh										
Primary	.70*	.30*	—	.44*	.11	.15			.16	.03
General	.62*	.49*	—	.15	—	.37*			.01	-.15

Table 4.10. (Page 2) Standardized Regression Coefficients: Factors in Council Candidate Electoral Success

City Election		Incumbency	Funds	NORC	SPAN	BLACK	Astan	Side[1]
Sacramento								
(137) Primary-After		.11	.14	.16*	-.03	.05	-.03	
(76) General-Before		.54*	.32*	.14	.10	—	—	
(20) General-After		.39*	-.07	—	-.31	—	—	
Peoria								
At-Large (95)	Primary	.33*		.33*				-.27
District (147)	Primary	.39*		.27*				-.27
Mixed (77)	Primary	.51*		.22*				-.09
At-Large (42)	General	.20		.08				-.29
District (62)	General	.29*		.16				—
Mixed (41)	General	.52*		.08				-.05
Des Moines								
(80) Primary-Before		.31*		.52*				—
(96) Primary-After		.47*		.27*				-.01
(59) General-Before		.10		.31*				-.24
(56) General-After		.50*		.22				.18

*Significant at the .05 level. Significance is present although these are not sample data, as an added dimension of the importance of the relationship.

**Variable does not enter into the equation.

[1]A "side of town" variable for cities where this is the most basic indicator of socioeconomic level of the constituency.

average spending levels and the importance of spending in election outcomes; although spending has been vitally important in San Antonio, it is only moderately so in Sacramento. It is highly important in all three Texas cities (in Dallas only since districts), which may reflect more organized patterns of spending there. (Lineberry 1977: 56)

Contrary to our hypothesis, there is no evidence that a district system serves to hold down the influence of money on election results. The coefficients for before and after the changes are not greatly different, and have increased in as many cases as they have gotten smaller. We have already seen that spending averages in mixed systems are lower for district than for at-large seats; we must conclude, however, that differences in the amounts spent by candidates for the same seat remain important predictors of success under the district system.

VOTER TURNOUT IN DISTRICT ELECTIONS

We have hypothesized that voter turnout will increase over levels found for at-large elections. However, predictions on the effect of districts on citizen interest in local government can plausibly predict either higher or lower levels of voting turnout. On the district side it can be argued that the individual will feel closer to politics in the district, will feel more effective in exercising the franchise, and will identify with the selection of a candidate who will be "his" voice at City Hall. The same citizen, it is said, if of an ethnic minority or from a lower income neighborhood, has been alienated from local government by a perception that at-large councils work for other interests. We will be testing predictions based on this argument.

The opposing view is that competition is almost automatic in at-large systems, since all that is required is one candidate more than there are seats. Come the district system, and an incumbent may discourage all competitors. Since that system provides that one's district—and perhaps one's racial or ethnic group will be represented, the incentive to exercise the franchise is *lessened* by district representation.

By introducing the discussion of findings on turnout, it is important to note a problem of intercity comparison. Electoral systems vary greatly at the local level, and the differences are reflected in our sample of cities. In most of them there is a two-step process, but in some (Charlotte, Raleigh) this is a primary/general procedure while in others it is a general election with a run-off, if the latter is needed to produce a majority victory. In Richmond, there is a single election, with outcomes decided on a pluralty basis. Charlotte has a partisan system, so primary figures may reflect a choice in only one party. Thus one cannot infer similar significance to turnout figures from the first and second election in the various cities.

There is an additional complication in comparing turnout in at-large and district elelctions. As suggested above, there is almost inevitably a choice on an at-large ballot for all voters. But in a district system, where incumbents are unopposed in some districts, should turnout be calculated citywide, or only for the contested districts? Our answer is to compute district-system turnout including and excluding uncontested districts, to see whether there is reason for this concern. Additionally, in mixed district/at-large systems we will compare the same districts in elections with and without district competition, to see whether district choice increases turnout levels for at-large seats.

Figures 4.3 and 4.4 show levels of turnout in council elections as a proportion of registered voters. Clearly, there is no consistent overall impact of structural change on participation in these elections. In most cases, particularly in first or primary elections, there is an increase in turnout in the first (D1) election after the change. This change is also evidenced in Peoria's primary after a shift from ten to five districts, which suggests that any structural change may temporarily heighten voting levels. Even more striking is the consistency of decline in turnout, back to at-large levels, from the first to the second district election. This temporary surge may be due in part to the novelty of a new electoral system. But it is more likely to be strongly influenced by the sudden appearance of seats without incumbents, and thus with an unusual number of competitive elections. There was only one uncontested districted contest in our ten cities in their first district elections; in 63 percent (45) of the districts, the winner received less than 60 percent of the vote. By the second district election, 20 percent of the seats were uncontested and over 70 percent were won with over 60 percent of the vote. Even though contested elections bring out voters, the institutionalization of an election system seems quickly to reduce competition, and thus, reduce turnout.

Our interest is not only in overall levels of turnout, however, but in identifying the relative importance of the factors that predict turnout under each system. These relationships can be examined more sensitively using multiple regression techniques. Table 3.10 shows the explanatory value of percent Hispanic or black, and of the average value of housing units in the census year closest to the election. We would expect as a normal pattern of voting behavior a positive slope on the relationship between house value and turnout, and a negative slope on the relationship between proportion minority and turnout. That is, each increase in income or decrease in proportion black or Hispanic should produce a

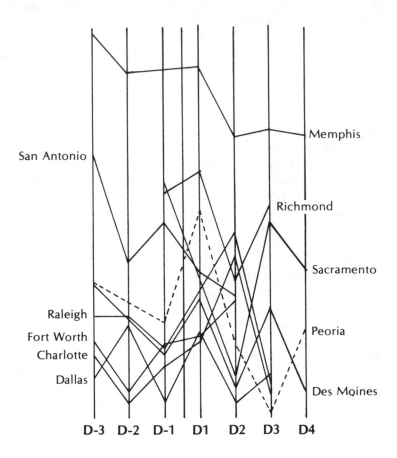

FIGURE 4.3. Turnout as Percentage of Registered Voters, First Election or Primary (Data unreliable for Montgomery; Peoria, going to more at-large system, shown by dotted line.)

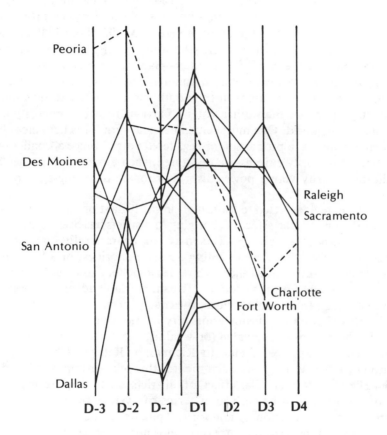

FIGURE 4.4 Turnout as Percentage of Registered Voters, Second Election or Run-Off. (No run-off elections in Richmond or predistrict Memphis'; data unreliable for Montgomery. Peoria, going to more at-large system, shown by dotted line.)

sizeable increase in turnout. If, on the other hand, the effect of districts is to heighten participation in lower-income or minority districts, these factors should be less predictive of turnout under districts.

The cities in Table 4.11 are arranged from highest to lowest in proportion minority. Through this spectrum, there is a consistent and positive relationship between house value and turnout, as expected, although its predictive power varies considerably. What may be surprising, however, is the seemingly random relationship between proportion minority and turnout in the at-large period. While about half of these cities show the predicted pattern, Charlotte, Raleigh, Richmond, Fort Worth, and—in the case of Hispanics—San Antonio show an at-large voting pattern of greater turnout in minority precincts. However, it is not uncommon in local elections in the South for miniorities to turn out in greater proportions than other voters, particularly when minority candidates are involved. One must remember that turnout is here measured as actual voters as a proportion of registered voters. Since a smaller proportion of minority citizens are registered, such a relationship does not indicate minority voting power disproportionate to voting-age population.

It is more unexpected to learn that, in the highest proportion minority city of Richmond, the effect of changing to districts has been to erase this minority turnout advantage. This may, of course, reflect greater increases in registration than in voting among minorities, or a ''dropping out'' from the rolls among those whites least inclined to vote. Likewise in San Antonio and Forth Worth, an Hispanic turnout advantage seems to have been lost. In most other cities, the change in structure seems to have had little effect on the turnout/minority relationship.

In the case of house value (or wealth), the change has more often produced the expected results. In Richmond, Raleigh, Charlotte, San Antonio, Forth Worth, and Sacramento, this relationship is reduced or even slightly reversed. The effect of districts on turnout seems much more consistently to be defined in terms of average precinct economic status than as a function of minority population. Thus, our hypothesis on the effect of districts on voter turnout is not supported in general, nor for minority voters examined separately. It is, however, somewhat validated as having a positive effect on less affluent voters.

Numbers do not tell the whole representation story. Minority district advocates sometimes feel that, even more important than the number and proportion of minority representatives is the freedom a district representative has to reflect the concens of his particular constituency. The minority representative elected with majority votes may not

Table 4.11. Mean Standardized Regression Coefficients of Turnout of Registered Voters, Before and After Districts, With Average House Value, Percentage Hispanic, and Percentage Black. (Units are precincts).

City	Average House Value Before/After	Percentage Hispanic Before/ After	Percentage Black Before/After
		Primary or First Elections	
Richmond	.72/.21		.41/.15
San Antonio	.55/-.23	.16/-.79	-.06/-.73
Charlotte	.49/.5(D) .36(AL)	—	.35/.80(D) .50(AL)
Dallas	.66/insuff. cases	—	.06/insuff. cases
Fort Worth	.48/-.17	.13/.30	.32/-.33
Memphis	.19/.12(D) .18(AL)	—	-.76/-.15(D) -.56(AL)
Montgomery	-.14/.09	—	-.75/-.21
Raleigh	.68/.60(D) .38(AL)	—	.55/.68(D) .65(AL)
Sacramento	.20/-.14	-.16/-42	-.13/-.15
Peoria	.51/.53(D) .62(AL)	—	-.13/.14(D) -.19(AL)
Des Moines	.39/.70(D) .63(D)	—	Side: -.15/.28(D) .07(AL)
		General or Run-Off Elections	
Richmond	—	—	—
San Antonio	.34/.70	-.06/.30	-.26/.16
Charlotte	.54/.62(D) .63(AL)	—	-.24/-.14(D) -.19(AL)
Dallas	.51/.46	—	.12/-.13
Fort Worth	.41/.43	.02/.14	.33/-.05
Memphis	.19/.12(D) .18(AL)	—	-.76/-.15(D) -.56(AL)
Montgomery	.04/.50	—	-.75/.02
Raleigh	.68/.62(D) .57(AL)	—	.63/.20(D) .14(AL)
Sacramento	.19/.02	.09/-.40	-.02/.10
Peoria	.65/.42(D) .62(AL)	—	-.26/-.32(D) -.24(AL)
Des Moines	.40/.70(D) .63(AL)	—	Side: -.15/.27(D) .07(AL)

act very differently than a white council member. This possibility fuels minority suspicion of the system where candidates are nominated by district but elected at large. We have seen that district representatives do not vary meaningfully in occupational status from those elected at large. Whether the district councilmembers behaves differently than his at-large counterpart is a central issue in the chapters to follow.

NOTES

1   See Reiss, 1961: 263–275. Duncan's index of socioeconomic status, found in the same source, was also calculated and correlated with electoral success. Since the two measures are highly interrelated (over .-9) in each population, only the NORC-based results are reported.

5

Representing the Constituency

AT THE HEART of most campaigns for public office are promises of "better" representation. It is rare, however, for candidates to clearly define their notion of representation or for them to identify the specific qualities which presumably make some cases of representation superior to others. On the other hand, beyond policy preferences based on economic or social interests, and outside of cliches about honesty, we have little knowledge of what any given aggregate of citizens (or voters) expects from a "good" representative.

As noted earlier, current scholarly attention to the concept of representation involves not only the trustee and delegate models, but also an ombudsman orientation. In brief, trustees base decisions on personal judgments of what will benefit the overall community, delegates act as instructed by constituencies, and ombudsmen service noncontroversial needs of individual constituents. Like all ideal models, these are not mirror images of any slice of reality; empirical studies have shown and common sense points to the fact that elected officials will be *primarily* trustees, delegates, or ombudsmen, not exclusively one of the three. Regardless, we found the models to be illustrative of identifiable styles of local representation, and thus quite valuable in categorizing the role orientations of council members in our eleven cities.

Our major interest, of course is not in merely categorizing council members, but in discovering whether representational styles are related to different kinds of constituencies, and, thus, to electoral structure. In the second chapter, we developed the following hypotheses concerning role orientations of district and at-large representatives:

1. District representatives identify themselves as ombudsmen or delegates while at-large members see themselves as trustees.
2. District members have more citizen-initiated contacts with constituents than do at-large members.

These hypotheses will be tested with information gathered through structured interviews with council members in our eleven cities. Our interview universe included those members who had served during the three terms preceding the change to districts and during all terms since the change. Complete interviews, somewhat limited in number by the availability of subjects, were conducted with seventy-one district and fifty-one at-large representatives; over three-fourths (77 percent) of the interviewees were members of post-district councils. Council members were asked, in an open ended format, to describe their roles; followup questions focused on their relationships with their constituents, especially in the processing of complaints. (The Council Member interview schedule is found in Appendix A).

Further, we expect district representation to affect the interactions of council members and city bureaucracies. Specifically, we hypothesized that

3. District representatives assume a more activist role in processing citizen complaints than do at-large representatives.
4. Administrators will perceive district representatives as more likely to interfere with administrative procedures.
5. District representatives will stress willingness to follow council direction as a desirable administrative trait; at-large members are more likely to favor a strong leadership role for the city manager.

To test these hypotheses, we will use the council members' interviews along with information obtained from interviews of forty-three city managers, assistant city managers, and department heads. Council members were asked to delineate their relationship with city managers and department executives. City officials were asked to describe the council/administration relationship from their perspective; questions stressed the handling of constituent complaints and the extent of council "interference" in administration. (The City Official interview schedule is found in Appendix A).

REPRESENTING URBAN CONSTITUENCIES: TRUSTEES, DELEGATES AND OMBUDSMEN

As we indicated in Chapter 2, the traditional meaning of the trustee concept and current usage of the ombudsman notion are easily adapted to urban settings. However, to make the delegate concept as useful as possible at the local level, it has been broadened to include the concern that specific geographic areas receive public goods and services in both sufficient quantity and acceptable quality.

Classifying our council members as trustees, delegates and ombudsmen shows quite clearly that at-large representatives and district representatives from affluent areas define their roles quite differently than do council members from the cities' poorer districts (See Table 5.1). Over 80 percent of the at-large members and nearly 90 percent of those from upper-income districts saw themselves as trustees; only 5 percent of the council members from the least affluent districts had this orientation.[1]

Looking only at district representatives, we find an extremely strong link between district wealth and representational style. While most upper-income and almost no lower-income representatives acted as trustees, slightly more than half of the middle-income representatives identified with that role. There were no ombudsmen among our members from relatively wealthy districts, while over half of those representing low-income districts acted according to that model. Another 40 percent of the low-income district representatives told us that their most important role was making sure their districts got a fair share of goods and services from the city. Several council members from these districts mentioned both taking care of personal problems and looking out for their area's share of city benefits as vital aspects of their job. Regardless of city or race, the men and women sent to council by their city's poorest voters gave descriptions of the councilmanic role infused with a sense of per-

Table 5.1. Role Orientation By Council Constituency

Orientation	Low Income	Middle Income	Upper Income	At-Large
Trustee	5.3	57.1	87.5	82.4
	(1)	(16)	(21)	(42)
Delegate	42.1	28.6	12.5	13.7
	(8)	(8)	(3)	(7)
Ombudsman	52.6	14.3	0.0	3.9
	(10)	(4)	(0)	(2)
	(19)	(28)	(24)	(51)

Significance = .0000

sonal responsibility for their constituents and for their part of the city. One of the three black district members elected to his city's first district council said that he wished to "change the image of government from something distant to where citizens can get legitimate concerns aired." Another new district representative saw his role as "[to] let people in my district know they have a representative to serve them and their interests." One city manager described the way in which a representative from a relatively poor district responds to complaints as follows: "He sees them (complaints) as *personal* matters, tracks down all the details and follows the activity personally . . . others (on the council) are more tolerant of the sometimes slow speed of the bureaucracy."

These feelings are quite different from those expressed by delegates from higher income areas and by district and at-large trustees. Some delegates from middle and upper income districts felt responsible for monitoring the performance of city services in their areas; others indicated a responsiveness to constituent views, especially on property issues such as taxes, zoning and streets. Trustees, however, whether elected at-large or by middle or upper income voters, had few, if any, particularistic concerns. Representatives from the wealthiest districts in several cities made comments such as ". . . people in my district don't need much" and ". . . they don't pay much attention [to the council], so I can afford to be interested in things outside the area." One at-large trustee who saw his most important role as "representing the city as a whole" argued that ". . . [at-large members] see the whole and reason and think issues out." Another said she ". . . will listen to who calls, but in the end must use my own best judgment . . . at-large members are elected to use their own judgement." Finally, another at-large trustee reported that while he talks to citizens who disagree with his policy stands and "tries to sell them", if he fails in such endeavors, he "goes in on his own."

Given these differing styles of representatives elected from varying constituencies, it is not surprising that our council members have contrasting perceptions of what interests their constituents. As indicated by Tables 5.2 and 5.3, both types of constituency and representational role orientation are significantly related to perceptions of constituent concerns. Members from lower- and middle-income districts are much more likely to believe that constituents are primarily concerned with district services and facilities or with individual problems. District representatives from wealthy areas are most likely to think constituents are interested in policy questions and in how the representative votes on issues before the council. However, as Table 5.2 shows, sizeable proportions of upper-income and at-large representatives do feel that their constituents

Table 5.2. **Perceptions of Constituent Concerns By Council Constituency**

Concerns	Constituency				
	Low Income	Middle Income	Upper Income	At-Large	Total
Votes/	5.6	10.0	50.0	31.3	26.1
Policy	(1)	(2)	(11)	(10)	(24)
District	44.4	55.0	13.6	18.8	30.4
Services/	(8)	(11)	(3)	(6)	(28)
Facilities					
Individual	44.4	30.0	27.2	28.1	31.5
Problems	(8)	(6)	(6)	(9)	(27)
Uncertain	5.6	5.0	9.2	21.8	12.0
	(1)	(1)	(2)	(7)	(11)
	(18)	(20)	(22)	(32)	(92)

Significance = .01

are mainly concerned with individual problems. Regardless of this perception, most at-large representatives in mixed councils felt that dealing with such problems was the job of district representatives, not their responsibility.

Similarly, it is the trustees who see a relatively large percentage of citizens concerned with policy issues and council votes (See Table 5.3). However, nearly half of the trustees acknowledge citizen concerns with district goods and services and with individual problems. That awareness does not lead trustees into a different representational style. We hesitate to describe our trustees as paternalistic;[2] we found most of them sincerely

Table 5.3. **Perceptions of Constituent Concerns by Role Orientations**

Concerns	Orientation		
	Trustee	Delegate	Ombudsman
Votes/Policy	34.0	21.7	6.2
	(18)	(5)	(1)
District	26.4	43.4	25.0
Services/	(14)	(10)	(4)
Facilities			
Individual	20.8	30.4	68.8
Problems	(11)	(7)	(11)
Uncertain	18.8	4.5	0
	(10)	(1)	(0)
	(53)	(23)	(16)

Significance = .01

interested in the betterment—as they defined it—of their cities and usually quite tolerant of opposing views on policy questions. Simply put, they did not wish to be "errand boys", no matter how many constituents might have errands to be run.

The relatively high level of uncertainty among trustees regarding constituent interests should also be noted. We would speculate that this is related to the fact that many trustees have only limited contact with their constituents, that is, the diverse groups of a large city. As one of the most thoughtful of our interviewees answered when asked about constituent concerns,

> we can never be sure about this, because we usually only hear from people who are angry or unhappy. How can we know what, if anything, concerns those people who don't get mad enough to call us?

Perceptions of delegates and ombudsmen are more in harmony with their representational styles. The emphasis on concerns about facilities, services and individual problems reported by delegates supports our impression that the *urban* delegate normally interprets his "orders from home" as "Take Care of the Neighborhood," not as instructions on council votes. Likewise, the subjective difference we discovered between delegates and ombudsmen—an emotional bond between the ombudsmen and "their people"—is also reflected in these findings, for nearly 70 percent of the ombudsmen believed that constituents were primarily concerned with personal problems needing a public solution.

Income, it seems to us, is the key variable in understanding how urban constituencies with district systems are being represented—council members select representational styles in line with the socioeconomic context of their district. Council members elected by affluent districts, as well as those elected at large, focus on "larger issues". While many of these members share the views and sometimes the objective interests of local businesses, they are rarely puppets of "the downtown". But most importantly, they do not feel that their service on council is linked to the *personal* needs of their constituents, for those constituents have few problems that local government can solve. For residents of affluent neighborhoods, then, being represented by someone elected by the district is quite similar to at-large representation. Residents of middle income districts fare somewhat differently under districts. A larger proportion of their council members choose representational styles that focus on the service needs of the district; it is our impression that such delegates are particularly concerned with services providing convenience and amenities. But it is the residents in the poorest areas for whom districts bring the most personalized and the most constant kind of attention. While critics might bemoan the "parochialism" and the errand-running of the lower-income representative, his constituents have the most errands to be run: They depend more than other citizens upon government for not only amenities but for many of the necessities of urban life. Thus, our hypothesis incorrectly linked representation of any district with an ombudsman role definition. It is only in less affluent districts where this relationship holds.

CONSTITUENT RESPONSE TO DISTRICTS: THE DISCOVERY OF THE OMBUDSMAN

We hypothesize more citizen-initiated contacts for district than for at-large representatives. Once districts are established, how do citizens respond to "their person at City Hall"? Council members were asked to estimate the number of times per week they were contacted by constituents concerning an individual problem. Table 5.4 demonstrates the effect of the change on at-large representatives before and after they were joined by district council members. For completely at-large councils (i.e., the predistrict councils) the range of contact frequency was enormous; some members performed the ombudsman role much more willingly than others. With the advent of mixed systems, however, most constituent contacts were redirected to district representatives. The median number of constituent service calls per week was fifteen for members of at-large councils; it drops to three for at-large members of mixed councils, compared to a median of twenty-five for the district members of those councils. Table 5.4 also indicates that representatives from districts with varying degrees of wealth receive different levels of constituent calls: The lower the district income level, the greater number of om-

Table 5.4. Frequency of Ombudsman Contacts Per Week By Constituency

Type	Max.	Min.	Mean	Median	N
Lower-Income District	250	3	61.3	25	14
Middle-Income District	100	2	31.1	22.5	16
Upper-Income District	70	2	18.3	10	15
At-Large, Pre-District	125	5	25.0	15	9
At-Large, Mixed Systems (current)	50	0	9.1	3	16
					(70)

budsman requests. In fact, representatives of upper income districts
received fewer constituent calls than at-large members of the predistrict
councils.

We do not, however, assume that district representatives passively
reflect their constituents' vision of the political process. Council
members, particularly those from lower-income areas, often advertise
themselves as ombudsmen, campaigning door-to-door as "the person
who can get things done for you at City Hall." One of the most
dedicated ombudsmen among our council members appears to give more
time to his constituent work than to his career as an insurance salesman.
He has spent years developing contacts, friendships and an outstanding
reputation among the residents of his district, and comes very close to being a model of what we would term an "aggressive ombudsman." What
is striking about our interviews is that we found a good number of council members who could be placed in such a category. In one illustrative
incident, an administrator recalled that one of his assistants was notified
of a complaint concerning loud motorcycles racing past a citizen's house
at night. An employee was dispatched to gether information on the complaint, much to the astonishment of the supposedly aggrieved citizen. "It
wasn't a big deal," the latter explained. "This woman came to the door,
identified herself as my council representative, and asked if I had any
complaints. That was the only thing I could think of." The perception on
the part of representatives that constituents are more interested in personal services than in policy questions is often reinforced by the constituent response which, in turn, was encouraged by the representative's
style.

Looking at the frequency of citizen-initiated contacts by representational style provides statistical evidence of such an interactive relationship. Comparing Tables 5.4 and 5.5 leads to the conclusion that style has
a stronger link to the frequency of service calls than district wealth.
While requests for assistance was higher for members from poor districts
than for other representatives, the difference between calls to ombudsmen and calls to other types of representatives is striking. Ombudsmen received double the mean number of calls made to delegates
and over four times the mean number made to trustees; the median for
contacts with ombudsmen is five times the median for the other two
styles.

Districts alone do not guarantee citizens an ombudsman. But where
districts have been recently established, the new opportunity to serve on
council has been taken by a substantial number of persons we have term-
ed "aggressive ombudsmen." And, as we have stated above, this type of
representative seems most likely to be found serving the poorest district

Table 5.5. Frequency of Ombudsman Contacts Per Week By Role Orientation

Role	Max.	Min.	Mean	Median	N
Trustee	125	0	18.8	10	31
Delegate	200	3	37.1	10	15
Ombudsman	250	15	78.6	50	14
					(60)

in a city. Our hypothesis on citizen-initiated contacts holds only with less-affluent constituencies.

INTERACTION WITH CITY ADMINISTRATORS

According to democratic theory, citizens contact representatives in order to inform them of policy preferences. In the preceding section, however, we found that only one-fourth of the council members interviewed felt that their policy positions or votes were of major interest to their constituents (See Table 5.2). On the other hand, the majority of our local representatives believed that either neighborhood facilities or services or the solution of individual problems were the major concern of those who elected them to council. If these perceptions are correct, newly adopted district systems seem vulnerable to tension and conflict whenever council members with aggressive, constituency-based styles, wishing to solve neighborhood or individual problems, come into contact with bureaucratic norms and procedures developed before the adoption of districts. In order to draw at least an outline of the relationship between district councils and city bureaucracies, we have looked at the manner in which our local representatives responded to citizen requests for assistance, at the reactions of administrators to council members' intervention into standard operating procedures, and, finally, at the way in which council members view the role of the city manager.

Response to Citizen Complaints

Once a citizen has placed a grievance in the hands of a representative, what happens to it? Professional administrators suggest that citizen requests can best be serviced if they are channeled through the city manager; statutes in city manager systems prohibit direct contact between elected officials and subordinate administrators. Yet a determined ombudsman may feel compelled to communicate with those who actually provide the services his constituents demand. We expect that district representatives will be more likely to take direct action in responding to citizen complaints, while at-large representatives will usually simply refer them to the manager's office.

Over 40 percent of the council members in our sample share two traits: They view themselves as trustees and they claim to operate only through the manager. We would expect these characteristics to be related; however, when we look at all other combinations of role perception and complaint process, there is an almost random spread of possible combinations. There are trustees who deal directly with city staff, and ombudsmen who work only through the manager. Likewise, there is no systematic difference between district and at-large representatives, or among representatives of more and less affluent districts.

The lack of a pattern in responding to citizens was one of the surprises discovered in our interviews. It is explained partly by the profusion of roles described by those who were members of at large councils: Some of them had carved out ombudsman roles before the manager system was well established in their cities, and never adapted to that political culture. As one long-time Charlotte council member put it, he "could decide as well as the manager what needed to be done." He felt it was "wrong when bureaucrats at any level aren't responsible to the public"—or more exactly, are not responsible to their representative.

Additionally, unlike the rest of the cities in this study, two have never operated under a council-manager system. Both Memphis and Montgomery went from a commission form of government to a strong-mayor system. Since commissioners are also heads of administrative units, one would expect a tradition where elected representatives would take care of constituent concerns themselves; there would be no one else to do it.

Interestingly, the absence of a city manager in Memphis and Montgomery does not appear to distinguish them in current council-administration relations. In Montgomery, council members report that the new mayor made it clear that constituent service calls should be referred to his executive assistant. Although some council members in that city refer minor matters (as defined by one of them, "those not involving money") to department heads, the transformation came quickly and seems as complete as in the cities with a manager system.

In Memphis, the break in direct relations between council members and lower echelon bureaucrats was slower in coming. Some representatives who served during the first two or three terms after districts apparently continued to operate in the commissioner mode; however, those who have served since 1971 report that newly elected mayor Wyeth

Chandler then insisted that service calls go through the Chief Administrative Officer. Although there has been some resistance to the change among senior council members, such resistance is not related to either district and at-large representatives, or to lower- and higher-income constituencies.

Finally, we find somewhat the reverse of preliminary expectations in Richmond, where members of the district council have been the strongest adherents to manager-system norms. In Chapter 3, we identified the most dramatic initial results of districts as the election of a black majority to the council, leading to the election of Henry Marsh as the first black mayor, the firing of the white city manager and his replacement by a black. With a black mayor and black manager, blacks believed that this was "their" system and have had no trouble working through either the manager's office or the Citizen's Assistance Office, an institutional ombudsman service, established under the previous at-large, majority-white council. According to our respondents, few lower-income minority citizens are aware of its existence, and when a council member introduces such constituents to the CAO, the citizens credit their representative with giving them access to an efficient channel for the solution of problems.

There does not appear, then, to be any link between form of representation and the manner in which complaints are processed by council members; our hypothesis is not supported by these findings.

Reactions of Administrators to Citizen-Initiated Council Intervention

Professional city administrators are socialized to reduce the "subjectivity" of rule-application processes through development of service delivery rules. According to Jones et al., (1978), such rules are "regularized procedures for the delivery of services, which are attempts to codify the productivity goals of urban service bureaucracies." These authors point out that there has traditionally been little room in the development of these rules for a "recipient satisfaction" factor; consequently, managers have usually responded to citizen complaints about service delivery only in terms of the consistency of rule application. Yet, service delivery rules have distributional consequences (Jones et al., 1978: 340).

If the at-large council is likened to a corporate board of trustees, and thus thought to avoid involvement in the application of delivery rules, the change to districts may have an effect on the council/manager relationship. We expected to find that managers would perceive more intervention in administrative matters from district representatives; in interviews with seven city managers and sixteen assistant managers and department heads, we sought to determine whether this hypothesis was correct.

All the managers report some difference in the demands of at-large and district representatives. At a minimum, this consisted of an increase in requests for information after district representatives joined the councils; in at least one city, additional staff were required to deal with council communications. In the most extreme cases, some managers feel that district representatives have tried to alter the decision rules to benefit their constituents and have attempted to get involved in administrative decisions. According to Jones et al., (1978: 341), although managers seem to accord some legitimacy to citizen satisfaction as a factor in service delivery, none are ready to admit their formulae are unfair, and thus are uniformly critical of efforts to reallocate benefits. On the other hand, whatever their private feelings, the managers we interviewed generally accept as legitimate the ombudsman role of council members mainly because it reduces citizen frustration with the channeling of complaints.

In at least two cities, administrators credit the district system with success in passing bond referenda. Charlotte voters defeated a referendum held during the last at-large council term to provide bonds for an expansion of the airport by 47 to 53 percent; voters on the west of the city, where the airport is located, turned the proposal down overwhelmingly, with 68 percent voting against it. Under the district council the plan came up again, and after west-side representatives had negotiated the shape of the bond package to their approval, they campaigned in favor of it among their constituents. This time, the vote on the west side was 58 percent in favor of the bonds, and the referendum passed on an overall 69 percent "yes" vote. In Fort Worth, a city official also volunteered that districts had helped in the passage of bond issues, in reducing the "us-them" attitude of minority voters to the proposals. The legitimacy of development funding among voters is extremely important to managers, and may offset annoyances they find in dealing with district representatives.

In the main, our data support the hypothesis that administrators will see district council members as more likely to interfere in administration.

Council Perceptions of the Manager's Role

If the change to district representation leads to more divergent expectations on how citizen initiatives will be processed, it may have a similar impact on the level of consensus concerning the manager's policy role. We predict that at-large representatives will approve of a strong leadership role for the manager, while district members will prefer a technician who will follow their orders.

City managers vary in the degree to which they initiate policy proposals. Some managers, as well as numerous mayors and council members, see the manager as merely the chief administrator, there to implement whatever policies the council adopts. But other managers take a more activist role, and they are expected to do so by many council members. Those who see the council as the public version of a corporate board of directors see the role of council members as part-time. In the extreme version of this perspective, the primary function of the council is to hire the manager; he should then be left free to "run the city," unless or until his overall performance is so inadequate that a replacement must be hired.

There is no necessary relationship, of course, between a member's electoral constituency—at large or district—and his preference as to the manager's role. But we have already seen that at-large members are more likely to define themselves as trustees, a view that corresponds with the "corporate image" of local government. Council members were asked if they knew of or could imagine situations where the manager was not sufficiently assertive. Forty-five percent of at-large representatives answered in the affirmative, compared to only 18 percent of district members (See Table 5.6). Among all ombudsman or delegate members, only thirteen percent could identify such a weak manager. Interestingly, only three of sixteen upper-income district representatives—most of whom are trustees—identified a weak manager situation; thus the critical factor here is at-large or district constituency, with role definition or constituency income having a secondary effect.

This analysis conforms to our city-by-city impression that the role definition of district representatives may conflict with the objectives of a manager who is a policy leader; that type of manager fits comfortably in

Table 5.6. Estimations of Assertiveness of Managers by Council Constituency

Perception That Manager Too Weak	Low Income	Middle Income	Upper Income	At-Large	Total
Yes	5.3	31.2	18.7	45.2	28.0
	(1)	(5)	(3)	(14)	(23)
No	94.7	68.8	81.3	54.8	72.0
	(18)	(11)	(13)	(17)	(59)
	(19)	(16)	(16)	(31)	(82)

Significance = .02

the at-large city, where council members are more likely to be trustees and more likely to expect the manager to provide policy leadership. These findings support our hypothesis.

COUNCIL AND CONSTITUENCY

Our findings concerning the link between lower-income constituencies and ombudsman role orientation have clear implications with regard to the access of citizens—including, of course, minorities—to local government. Most at-large council members do not wish to deal with individual problems, even though they recognize that these are what concern many constituents. Furthermore, an administrator candidly stated that lower-income citizens in particular had not called on the wealthy members of his city's at-large council for assistance because they would feel uneasy about making such calls. Several council members from lower-income areas also suggested that their constituents had been hesitant to call city hall prior to district representation because they felt that city employees would treat them in a condescending manner.

District representation has provided residents of the poorer areas in all our cities with council members eager to help with individual, immediate problems that involve city services or facilities. It is also clear that these council members believe that districts have improved local government by giving their part of the city a "voice at city hall." Finally, evidence from a survey conducted in Charlotte[3] three-and-a half years after districts were initiated supports the claim that minority citizens will be pleased with this type of representation: 66 percent of black Charlotteans felt that city government has improved since the change in electoral structure, whereas only 37 percent of the white respondents agreed with this assessment.

Whether this perceived improvement is generally related to larger questions of city policy is questionable. In a situation such as Richmond's, where districts led to a black-majority council and thus a black mayor, all areas of city policy were affected. When, on the other hand, representatives of minority or low-income districts remain a council minority, their impact will probably be limited to the ombudsman and delegate activities.

NOTES

1   The use of census-based house values as surrogate measures for average income is described in the note on Table 3.6.

2   Eulau and Prewitt (1973: 407–411) suggest that the majority of the Bay Area councils they studied had trustee orientations with an underlying "current of paternalism." They were, however, speaking of entire councils, almost all elected at-large, not about individual trustees in mixed or district systems.

3   Data From a telephone survey conducted by the Institute for Urban Studies, University of North Carolina at Charlotte, in October, 1980. A sample of 850 adults was drawn by random digit dialing.

6

Actions of District Councils: Agenda-Setting and Decision-Making

IN THE LAST CHAPTER we were concerned with individual styles of representation and with constituent responses to district representatives. We turn now to investigate the more formal proceedings of our councils, both before and after the adoption of districts; we will focus on the questions of whether and how district representation affects council proceedings.

We have suggested earlier that the presence of members with geographically and socially distinct constituencies will influence both the topics included on council agendas and the extent of conflict evoked by council decisions. We hypothesize, first, that there will be more controversy in council proceedings after the adoption of districts. This change in the level of consensus found in council deliberations should occur both generally and in the specific policy areas of redistribution and social services, public safety and zoning and planning. As we noted in the second chapter, we expect disagreements over what we call social minimum issues between council members from predominantly minority and low-income districts and those from more affluent areas. Similar disagreements may occur over questions of public safety, especially those pertaining to law enforcement. Conflicts between developers, other advocates of continuing urban expansion and residents of middle income neighborhoods should be reflected by council controversy over matters of zoning and planning. There should also be increased levels of disagreement over internal questions of decision-making procedures, especially when decisions concern personnel and power over the budgetary process. Further, we predict that the presence of representatives with heterogeneous electoral bases will result in the emergence of voting coalitions based on race, ethnicity, and district demographics. Finally, we predict that the concerns of district members with the quantity and quality of services provided in their neighborhoods will result in postdistrict agendas giving increased attention to routine services.

We believe that each of these changes in council proceedings will accompany either a complete change to an all-district council or the introduction of district seats into at-large councils. In other words, we do not expect the direction of our findings to depend on the proportion of district seats in any of the councils, but simply on the presence or absence of district representatives. Because our deviant case, Peoria, added at-large seats to a district council, it will not be included in this chapter's analyses.

DATA ON COUNCIL PROCEEDINGS

Analyses will be based on council minutes and on roll call votes.[1] In order to utilize these data sources, it was necessary to aggregate agenda items into categories which are both conceptually meaningful and empirically useful. Our categories begin with those developed by Lucy, Gilbert, and Burkhead (1977). Briefly, Lucy et al. classified municipal services as routine (traffic and waste disposal, for example), protective (public safety), developmental (recreation, education), and social minimum (welfare programs). To fully capture the wide variety of topics normally included on council agendas, we added four categories: regulation of economic activity (e.g., granting of licenses), financial issues not clearly linked to one substantive policy area (e.g., approval of budgets as prepared by city managers), symbolic topics, and the structure/process category.

Most of our findings will be based on roll call votes taken during council meetings before and after changes to districts. However, for those cities where council records were available in verbatim form, we will also employ interaction analysis to study the effects of districts on the activities of local legislatures.

INTERACTION ANALYSIS OF COUNCIL PROCEEDINGS

Sociologists and social psychologists have developed a number of techniques for studying the formal interactions of small groups. However, except for coalition formation analysis and reports of congressional committee behavior, political scientists have rarely studied small group interactions. Eulau and Prewitt (1973) identified categories of council interactions and governing styles, but these categorizations were based on interviews of council members, not on actual interactions.

Here, council interactions will be examined through an application of content analysis to council minutes; this approach was inspired by Bales' Interaction Process Analysis (1950, 1970), first utilized in political science in Barber's (1966) study of local finance committees. The technique was modified by Walcott and Hopmann (1978) to provide categories of statements according to their function in the decision-making process, and was labeled Bargaining Process Analysis. Three BPA categories are relevant to our purpose here:

1. *Initiations*: Actor advances a substantially new proposal or states his own substantive position for the first time. Initiation in formal council settings usually consists of the introduction of a topic in a staff report or in a council member's motion or amendment.
2. *Agreements:* Expressions of substantive agreement with another's position. The seconding of motions was automatically coded as agreement, as were most additional expressions of support.
3. *Disagreements:* The rejection of another's proposal, or dispute with another's position or explanation.

For coding purposes, each uninterrupted statement by a participant in a council meeting is considered a unit of analysis.

One of the consequences of our application of interaction analysis to a nonexperimental, "real-world" setting is that the use of minutes as data is equivalent to applying a form of content analysis to these written records. Walcott and Hopmann designed BPA to be applicable either to verbal interaction or to transcripts thereof, and Hopmann's 1974 application is from transcripts. Transcript analysis avoids several problems inherent in the simultaneous coding of ongoing exchanges: Judgments need not be instantaneous, and can be more thoughtful; coders' reliability can easily be checked; and a uniform and comprehensive system of interval sampling of interactions can be applied over extended periods of time, a crucial point in the present study.

Since interaction analysis makes sense only if applied to records that are near verbatim, our use of this technique is limited to the cases of Charlotte, Raleigh, and San Antonio.[2]

LEVELS OF COUNCIL CONFLICT

We have shown in the preceeding chapter that council members representing less affluent districts have different role orientations than members elected from wealthier districts or by the city at-large. We also expected representatives with contrasting constituencies to have different priorities which would, in turn, be manifest in disagreements over council actions. In brief, we hypothesized that the adoption of districts would introduce new conflicts into council deliberations, disrupting the consensual operations of at-large assemblies. Operationally, we expected to find higher levels of disagreement in interactions, and far greater proportions of nonunanimous, contested roll call votes after district members joined our councils.

OVERALL CONFLICT

Evidence on proportion of disagreements (see Table 6.1) does not offer strong support for the expectation of conflict under districts. In the three councils examined, and in all four time periods, disagreement as a proportion of total communications does not exceed 7.5 percent. In San Antonio, the proportion remains constant throughout the period under study. In Charlotte there was a steady rise in disagreement, but certainly not a striking transformation. Although patterns in Charlotte and Raleigh are as predicted, the numbers are too small and the changes too gradual to suggest that district councils are more contentious.

The analysis of split votes in Table 6.2 makes clear that most of our councils fit the "old boy" stereotype during the two at-large terms prior to the move to districts. The two exceptions, Charlotte in the D–2 term and Richmond in both terms, are linked to unique situations. The D–1

Table 6.1. Percentage of Disagreements in Council Interactions

City	D – 2	D – 1	D1	D2
Charlotte	0.9	1.3	3.3	—
Raleigh	2.8	5.1	6.4	7.5
San Antonio	5.7	6.3	5.4	5.0

Table 6.2. Split Votes As Percentage of Council Votes

Term	Charlotte	Des Moines	Fort Worth	Memphis	Montgomery	Raleigh	Richmond
D-2	7.7 (17/2205)	1.7 (3/173)	3.3 (125/3839)	0.0 (0/133)	—	2.8 (96/3423)	23.5 (90/383)
D-1	15.0 (259/1728)	8.7 (18/207)	5.6 (311/4769)	2.1 (4/188)	0.9 (20/2104)	4.6 (172/3705)	27.6 (135/490)
D1	15.0 (380/2533)	32.0 (107/334)	5.0 (295/5910)	3.2 (5/154)	11.7 (153/1304)	3.4 (142/4086)	12.8 (72/562)
D2	15.7 (162/1031)	28.5 (101/351)	2.4 (179/7520)	6.3 (8/128)	—	9.2 (326/3525)	8.1 (45/555)

Charlotte council marked a turning point in the socioeconomic makeup of that city's representatives; during the term, relatively young professionals began to replace owners of small businesses and executives as the council's dominant occupational group. This "modernization" which occurred two years prior to the district referendum was largely responsible for the increase both in interaction disagreements and in contested votes during the D-1 term.

The Richmond data presented in Table 6.2 contradict not only our prediction of increased conflict, but also the assumption of consensus in at-large councils. Not only do split votes as a percentage of total votes decrease with the advent of districts, but approximately one-fourth of the roll calls in the predistrict councils resulted in split votes. Here we encounter a problem inherent in quantitative analysis of voting in small groups: A single member, consistently voting by himself, can have a substantial effect on the overall rate of dissent. In the last few at-large councils in Richmond, Howard Carwile was the only member not elected through the "establishment-selected" TOP slate. Rather, he campaigned as a populist opponent of the TOP elite, and won a seat among them. They responded by denying him committee positions, and they left him out of informal deliberations. He reacted by casting lone dissents on a wide variety of issues. Although this had a substantial effect on the overall dissent level, the at-large council was, for decision-making purposes, highly consensual. This can be seen in Table 6.3, where the solo votes of the most frequent dissenter are shown as a percentage of all split votes in each term. In predistrict Richmond, over half of all split votes were Carwile's lone dissents. After districts, the percentage of split votes resulting from the most frequent single dissenter fell to 21 percent. Subtracting splits caused by the most important lone dissenter on each council changes the percentage of split votes in that city to 10.5 in D-2, 12.7 in D-1, 10.1 in D1, and 6.5 in D2.

Only two of the seven cities experienced the predicted consequences

Table 6.3. Percentage of All Split Votes Resulting From
Lone Dissenting Votes Cast by The Most Frequent Lone Dissenter

Term	Charlotte	Des Moines	Fort Worth	Raleigh	Richmond
D-2	23.7	70.6	15.6	11.0	53.4
D-1	24.0	33.3	6.2	29.3	54.5
D1	4.0	23.1	18.7	15.5	20.8
D2	6.0	29.0	10.5	11.9	20.5

(Montgomery had a 3-member commission before districts; on that size body, calculations of "lone dissents" wold be meaningless.)

of district representation: the level of conflict escalated in the Des Moines and Montgomery councils immediately after the adoption of districts, and remained at a high level during the D2 term in Des Moines. As seen in Table 6.2, that city's council changed abruptly from a consensual body with only rare disagreements to a group that split on nearly a third of its votes once districts were established. What is more, the dissenting voters were usually the two council members from the blue-collar east side, the area that had given strongest support to district representation. Geographic and class conflict, which had been festering in Des Moines for decades, was brought into a formal arena by district representation, and the east-side coalition continued until at lest the second term after the adoption of districts.

Although the rate of increase of council conflict was greater in Montgomery than in Des Moines, the absolute percentage of postdistrict split votes—nearly 12 percent—remained rather low in the Alabama city. In the at-large period, Montgomery had the smallest governing body among those under examination here, a three member commission. "Establishment" candidates were selected as a slate by leaders of the business community, and these teams invariably won the elections. In this setting, on a body of just three members, with each commissioner predisposed to support the others on votes covering their areas of administrative jurisdiction as a reciprocal courtesy, it is hardly surprising that open, formal conflict (as recorded in a split vote, for example) would be extremely rare. Even in the final at-large term, when Mayor Robinson was campaigning against his two colleagues to replace the commission wiht a mayor-council system, their disagreements rarely extended to roll-call voting. Montgomery politics since districts has seen considerable controversy roughly along racial lines, but Mayor Folmar, as a forceful leader in a strong-mayor system, has been able to keep council voting dissent to a minimum. He rewards cooperation, has a good working relationship with the white members of the council, and makes it costly for black members to vote against his proposals with consistency. The change in Montgomery from at-large to districts provided the basis for increased dissent in accordance with our prediction; however, the simultaneous change from a commission to a strong mayor seems to have served to mute that dissent rather effectively.

The only other increase in split voting and interaction disagreement after districts is found in Raleigh's D2 council. Most of the first district council had, in the words of a Raleigh *News and Observer* editorial (November 8, 1973) represented "widespread citizen resistance to urban growth. . . . The new council is probably going to say 'no' to many of the kinds of rezoning requests previously approved." Development interests had been blitzed, for no incumbents were re-elected except for the black member who returned as mayor; only two of the seven members even moderately supported the developers. One new member exulted that "This is the end of a long prodeveloper era," and saw the election as a "citizen revolt" against the council being run by the economically powerful interests of the city. Thus, the new council acted in a state of relatively euphoric consensus.

On the other hand, a defeated candidate, said to represent business interests, was quoted as remarking that "we, the conservatives, had better go to work on our political activities. The liberals are lean and hungry." The D2 council saw the only proneighborhood at-large member replaced by a business-supported candidate, and mayor Clarence Lightner was defeated for reelection by a developer. This brought the council into roughly equal balance between the two factions, and set the stage for heightened conflict, especially as the business interests began to push for the creation of an additional at-large seat.

While the evidence is certainly mixed, it does not provide strong support for the prediction that the proceedings of district and mixed councils will generally be marked by high levels of contested votes.

Conflict Over Questions of Social Assistance

We predicted that representatives of low income districts would become embroiled in disputes with their colleagues over issues of redistribution and social welfare, the issues we have labeled "social minimum" votes. Such a pattern is found most vividly in Montgomery, where no votes on social minimum issues were contested during the D-1 term, but divisions were found in 30 percent of such votes in the first district council (See Table 6.4).

Such a change might not have been predicted for the Alabama capital from our Chapter 3 discussion of the change to districts, for the plan had been adopted largely as a result of dissatisfaction with commission government, not as a response to minority pressure. But the change was our most dramatic structurally, from what was really a plural executive of three members chosen as an at-large slate, to a district plan that reflected the income and racial extremes as distributed geographically in a deep-south city. There were no white neighborhood groups involved in this case, so that one would expect an increase in conflict to fall precisely in the area of social assistance. Additionally, Community Development Block Grants became available during the D1 term, giving potential contenders something of value as a basis for disagreement.

However, none of the other cities provides evidence to suggest that

Table 6.4. Split Votes As Percentage of Votes on Social Minimum Issues

Term	Charlotte	Des Moines	Fort Worth	Memphis	Montgomery	Raleigh	Richmond
D-2	13.6 (11/81)	0.0 (0/2)	15.3 (2/13)	0.0 (0/1)	—	0.0 (0/50)	36.8 (7/19)
D-1	7.5 (5/67)	50.0 (2/4)	5.9 (2/34)	0.0 (0/1)	0.0 (0/37)	10.7 (8/75)	9.1 (2/22)
D1	13.8 (19/38)	56.7 (17/30)	14.3 (11/17)	0.0 (0/1)	30.0 (21/70)	1.8 (2/114)	0.0 (0/15)
D2	20.7 (12/58)	30.6 (15/49)	13.6 (8/59)	0.0 (0/3)	—	3.0 (4/133)	15.3 (3/20)

such an increase in conflict was widespread in cities adopting districts. In Des Moines, neither the increased attention to social minimum issues nor the high levels of conflicts over those issues was related to district representation in the expected manner. Des Moines began considering its participation in the Model Cities program in 1968, the first year of the new council; the number of votes on social minimum issues increased due to initiatives for participation coming from the city manager and his staff, not from the council. The high proportion of split votes in this category can be linked to district representation, but the east-siders—the representatives from the least affluent districts—frequently opposed the bureaucrats' plans for Model Cities. Since Des Moines has such a low proportion of blacks, and since the black population was not concentrated in the least affluent district, this outcome is not particularly surprising.

Richmond shows a pattern contrary to that predicted, with a drastic reduction in the level of social minimum splits with the change to districts. We have previously explained the high level of split voting in predistrict Richmond as the result of a single lone dissenter, Howard Carwile, who opposed the council leadership in all issue areas. That explanation extends to this particular area as well. In the other cities under consideration, the change to districts did not result in a complete realignment of forces as witnessed in Montgomery, Des Moines, and Richmond, but rather in a shift in the relative strength of groups represented. It is not surprising, then, that the proportion of split votes in this area does not reflect a quantum change from the shift in representation.

CONFLICT OVER PUBLIC SAFETY

A frequent point of conflict in urban politics has been the orientation of the police and other protective and enforcement agencies toward minorities. Our assumption was that such concerns would surface in the proceedings of district councils. Yet the council with voting patterns most in line with our hypothesis was that of Des Moines, a council without minority members in a city with very few minority residents. The increase in split votes in the public safety category shown in Table 6.5 is in fact related to conflicts over public safety personnel matters, especially a contract dispute between the city administration and a fire-fighters' association.

Of the councils with increased black representation, Montgomery and Fort Worth come closest to the hypothesized behavior. The proportion of split votes on public safety issues increased from 11.4 to 37.2 per-

Table 6.5. Split Votes as Percentage of Votes on Public Safety Issues

Term	Charlotte	Des Moines	Fort Worth	Memphis	Montgomery	Raleigh	Richmond
D-2	4.0 (4/126)	6.7 (1/15)	17.9 (5/28)	0.0 (0/0)	—	3.5 (9/259)	15.6 (5/32)
D-1	23.4 (22/94)	24.0 (6/25)	11.4 (4/35)	10.0 (2/20)	0.0 (0/298)	2.4 (7/283)	17.4 (14/23)
D1	16.2 (22/135)	57.1 (20/35)	37.2 (16/43)	0.0 (0/2)	8.4 (12/143)	1.4 (10/711)	5.3 (2/38)
D2	8.3 (6/72)	48.8 (21/43)	12.5 (5/40)	0.0 (0/5)	—	4.9 (21/429)	11.8 (4/34)

cent betwen Fort Worth's D-1 council and its first district body. Examination of the votes at issue, however, indicate that most of them concerned the location and construction of headquarters and support facilities, and did not involve either the geographic distribution of protective services or the manner in which those services were provided. However, the proportion of contested votes fell back to the predistrict level in the second term after districts. Montgomery shows a less dramatic increase in disagreements over protective issues; there were no split votes during the predistrict term compared to 8.4 percent during the first postdistrict council. The hypothesized voting pattern was not found in Charlotte, Memphis, Raleigh or Richmond. If there was dissatisfaction with protective services among the minority populations of any of these cities, it was not of a nature that suggested controversial public policy solutions.

Conflict Over Zoning and Planning

This issue area has the potential for bringing developers, realtors and other businesses with interests in downtown redevelopment or residential expansion into conflict with neighborhood groups that have gained representation on district councils. But again, only Des Moines and Montgomery show changes in the direction of our predictions. As shown in Table 6.6, splits on zoning and planning in the Des Moines council increased from 2.4 percent in the D-1 council to 17.7 percent at D1 and remained considerably higher than pre-district levels (13.3 percent) at D2. Many of these votes were concerned with downtown redevelopment projects, one of many points of contention between the east side district representatives and the city bureaucracy. Disagreements in the Des Moines council often focused upon recommendations made by the city manager, recommendations which were frequently opposed by the east siders and supported by most or all of the other council members. It is impossible to say how much of the conflict in this policy area was substantive and how much was symbolic. Certainly the east-side districts, and particularly the poorest areas of one of them, were in need of additional and improved public facilities and services. However, since most of the downtown projects combined federal urban renewal money with private capital, these were not either/or—either spend money on downtown or on the east side—decisions. In Montgomery, much of the conflict in this policy area can be explained in terms of a mayoral coalition we will describe in the next section.

Neither Richmond nor Fort Worth experienced any increase in conflict over planning and zoning after adoption of districts. These cities did

Table 6.6. Split Votes As Percentage of Votes on Zoning and Planning

Term	Charlotte	Des Moines	Fort Worth	Memphis	Montgomery	Raleigh	Richmond
D-2	20.3 (37/180)	1.2 (1/82)	14.7 (34/230)	0.0 (0/40)	—	8.3 (42/508)	27.3 (24/88)
D-1	28.7 (69/240)	2.4 (2/82)	28.7 (80/289)	0.0 (0/89)	1.4 (10/730)	9.9 (66/666)	14.9 (7/47)
D1	26.3 (30/114)	17.7 (19/113)	29.9 (90/301)	0.0 (0/43)	10.4 (51/489)	5.2 (39/745)	9.3 (7/75)
D2	15.0 (24/160)	13.3 (10/75)	18.2 (68/373)	10.5 (6/57)	—	13.1 (83/636)	10.0 (9/90)

not have planning and zoning on the agenda of conflict over representation, and in the absence of some developer/neighborhood incident would not be expected to focus on this subject as a result of districts. In fact, questions of urban redevelopment in downtown Richmond were handled very consensually between Mayor Marsh and the city's commercial interest; both saw benefits for their constituencies in a surge of construction, whether in employment or investment.

Memphis, although it does not show an immediate increase in split votes on zoning and planning issues, went from no split votes on this subject before or in the first term after districts, to six of fifty-seven in the sample of D2 votes. However, there is no reason to believe that district representation is related to this change.

It is in Charlotte and Raleigh that zoning and planning were a major focus of the dissatisfaction which led to districts. In Charlotte, however, disagreement in these areas had been common since the introduction of a new generation of council members in the D-1 period. This level of conflict remained high into the D1 period, dropping off in D2 only with the resolution of some of the problems separating development interests from neighborhood organizations. In a later discussion the effects of districts on the relative strengths of these forces will be examined, but the level of dissent can only be said to have been part of the same stream of conflict that brought districts to Charlotte. Raleigh, like Memphis, shows an increase in conflict on planning and zoning in the D1 period. Our earlier discussion of general levels of conflict in Raleigh focused on this policy area as defining that city's contending forces. Nor surprisingly, the increase in conflict during the second district term coincides with a similar increase in the overall level of split voting: The first district council was so predominantly neighborhood-oriented that conflict only rose to its full potential when development interests regained ground in the next election.

Conflict Over Matters of Structure and Process

When we turn to roll call votes on questions concerning the relationship between our cities' councils and their bureaucracies, the administration of city departments, and other matters that turn about power and personnel, we once again find the predicted pattern of behavior only in Des Moines and Montgomery. Table 6.7 shows that when Des Moines established district seats on its council, patterns of voting on these questions changed immediately. The increase in proportion of split votes was spectacular, as it escalated from none during the two terms before districts to nearly 70 percent in the first district council. And while the

Table 6.7. Split Votes As Percentage of Votes on Structure Process

Term	Charlotte	Des Moines	Fort Worth	Memphis	Montgomery	Raleigh	Richmond
D–2	6.5 (16/245)	0.0 (0/18)	66.7 (10/15)	0.0 (0/8)	—	4.8 (13/271)	24.7 (19/77)
D–1	19.8 (24/121)	0.0 (0/14)	50.0 (30/60)	0.0 (0/3)	2.0 (6/299)	11.8 (25/211)	28.9 (24/83)
D1	8.1 (19/236)	69.8 (30/43)	38.8 (52/154)	0.0 (0/19)	17.4 (26/149)	13.2 (20/190)	17.0 (15/88)
D2	6.6 (5/76)	29.8 (14/47)	20.9 (18/86)	0.0 (0/3)	—	24.9 (85/342)	8.8 (11/125)

proportion of contested votes drops to around 30 percent in the next term, a sample of roll calls taken during the second district council again shows extremely high levels of conflict over questions of administration and personnel: Over half of the votes on structure and process in that term were split. What is more, a sample of votes cast during the *fifth* post-district council also supports the claim of ongoing conflict over structure/process issues: in that term, 40 percent of those votes were contested. Our findings in the case of Des Moines are not surprising. Conflict over manager government was at the core of Des Moines politics for over two decades; district representation gave opponents of both manager government and of two incumbent managers a forum for voicing and voting this position. The extraordinarily high levels of split votes over matters of power and personnel are directly related to the context of Des Moines politics. As in Des Moines, the first district council in Montgomery did not just strengthen the voices of previously under-represented groups, it added them for the first time. Thus there is a parallel situation in which virtual unanimity in the at-large period gives way to vigorous discussion of procedures and staffing under a new form of government.

In contrast, decisions concerning administration and personnel became more consensual after districts in Charlotte, Fort Worth, and Richmond. Discussions about establishing districts had been internal to these councils in the final at-large terms and the general subject became less important after the representation issue had been decided. All votes on these topics by the Memphis council during the four terms studied were unanimous. Once again, divisions were more common in Raleigh's second district council, when the city's commercial and development leaders introduced proposals to increase the proportion of at-large representation.

Districts and Levels of Conflict

There is clearly no simple relationship between district representation and the level of conflict on councils. While the change to districts in some cases and for some subject matters did affect the level of conflict, our hypothesis was not generally supported. The effect depends on whether representatives of entirely new interests are introduced into the council, and whether particular policy areas are relevant to the newcomers' constituents. To further define the relationship, we must turn to the relationship between council composition and council voting patterns.

COUNCIL COALITIONS

Even though district representation does not automatically result in increased levels of conflict during formal council proceedings, the presence of district members might still affect patterns of voting on those questions that are not decided unanimously. Also, where there were indications of increased conflict under districts, our explanation of the change must ultimately rest on a verification of the source of dissent. We predicted that the adoption of districts would result in the emergence of council blocs based on race, ethnicity or district demographics. To explore this topic, we have analyzed roll-call data from six of our cities.

The context in which one searches for coalitions should be shaped by the dynamics that led to the adoption of districts. In one city of this subset, Richmond, district adoption was linked to racial issues. In Des Moines, on the other hand, the district experience was related to long-standing resentments and misunderstandings between the white-collar and blue-collar sides of the city. Montgomery adopted districts as the price to be paid for black assent to, and Justice Department approval of, a referendum to change from a commission to a strong-mayor system. Forth Worth's district movement included a racial element along with liberal opposition to the power of downtown business interests. Finally, the motivations of district advocates in Charlotte and Raleigh stemmed from the interests and frustrations of neighborhood groups.

Coalition patterns which emerged in Richmond and Des Moines are clearly in the direction we expected. On the other hand, coalition parameters in Charlotte, Montgomery, Fort Worth, Raleigh are less clear and cannot as easily be explained by the adoption of districts.

Richmond: Voting By Racial Bloc

The election of five blacks to Richmond's nine-seat council completely changed the voting patterns of that city's legislature. In predistrict terms, TOP-endorsed members, often including the black councilman who became mayor under the new system, had high levels of unanimity. Only Richmond's lone dissenter disagreed with his colleagues with any frequency or consistency. As Table 6.8 shows, the first district council had two easily identifiable coalitions. One, labeled the TOP bloc, consisted of three of the four TOP-backed candidates in the 1977 election. Although the perceptions of many participants, the local press and other observers are that this council almost always voted in 5–4 racial blocs, our matrix indicates that the representative from the newly annexed **area (District 4) often disagreed with other white members. Somewhat**

Table 6.8. Percentage Agreement on Split Votes, Richmond Term D1 (N = 72)

	Majority White*			Swing			Majority Black		
	4	1	9	2	5	6	3	7	8
4	X	54	24	44	39	17	20	20	21
1		X	83	80	29	59	52	61	62
9			X	83	39	68	74	68	68
2		Top Bloc		X	32	63	67	66	60
5					X	65	59	62	60
6						X	97	97	97
3				Marsh Bloc			X	97	97
7								X	96
8									X

similarly, the black representing the "swing" district (District 5) was not always part of the black coalition, the group labeled MARSH BLOC on Table 6.8. However, race was clearly the dominant factor in coalition formation on this council. Not only does it describe voting in the aggregate, but two crucially important questions were decided by racial bloc votes. At the beginning of the D council, Henry Marsh was chosen Richmond's mayor by the 5–4 margin, and the next year the firing of the incumbent city manager was approved in a similar manner. The strength of the Marsh faction should also be noted; its four members voted together on almost all split votes during the first district council.

Following the 1978 election, the Fifth District representative, returned to council by the voters in his swing district, moved into the Marsh bloc; his voting record becomes extremely similar to those of all other black members except the mayor (See Table 6.9). On the other hand, only remnants of a TOP bloc remain. In fact, a liberal white appointed to fill a vacancy by the mayor (District 2), could easily be placed in the Marsh coalition. She, in turn, was overwhelmingly defeated by the former city manager in the 1980 election.

There is little doubt that race was the major factor in divisions on the Richmond council during the first two district terms. While the racial split may not be as constant as observers and even most members perceive it to be, its true extent along with those perceptions point unequivocably to racially-based voting as the dominant feature of the Richmond district council. The defeat of Henry Marsh and concomitant selection of another black councilman as mayor by a 5–4 majority comprised of four whites and the new mayor suggest two things: white

Table 6.9. **Percentage Agreement on Split Votes, Richmond Term D2 (N = 45)**

	4	1	9*	2**	5	6	3	7	8
4	X	73	53	56	39	45	42	42	58
1		X	44	82	53	68	61	65	62
9	Remnants of Top		X	48	39	49	39	36	36
2	Bloc			X	75	73	83	72	73
5					X	91	93	68	88
6						X	95	89	97
3			Marsh Bloc				X	85	94
7								X	92
8									X

* Nonincumbent
** Appointed to fill vacancy by mayor

members may be once again forming a strong, consistent voting block and they appear willing to bring blacks into that coalition to form a council majority. It seems safe to predict that Richmond's district representatives will continue to split along racial lines for at least as long as four white members are elected to the council.

Des Moines: Two Sides of Town

We have previously shown that the Des Moines council changed from a consensual to a conflictual body after the adoption of districts. As Tables 6.10 and 6.11 clearly show, at-large and west side representatives had frequent disagreements with the two east side members. What is more, this clear-cut division was found consistently in votes on all policy issues considered by the council.

It should be noted, however, that the two "first generation" east siders were not carbon copies of one another; they differed in personality, political style and to some degree in political goals. One, labeled "East Side 2" in our tables, was more the conservative ideologue, and more extreme in his distrust of and dislike for city administrators, "liberals," and persons usually called an "establishment." "He shook people up," was a frequent description of this man who was applauded as a hero by many on his side of the river, but viewed as an irrational troublemaker by many opponents. "East Side 1" on the other hand, spoke more and more softly after joining the council as he became more and more skilled

Table 6.10. Percentage Agreement on Split Votes,
Des Moines, Term D1 (N = 107)

	At-Large		Districts			
	AL1	AL2	West Side 1	West Side 2	East Side 1	East Side 2
AL1	X	79	88	75	45	15
AL2		X	72	61	41	23
WS1			X	80	48	23
WS2				X	37	21
ES1					X	68
ES2						X

at working with mayors, council colleagues and city bureaucrats in order to gain benefits for his constituents. It is not inconceivable, of course that this serendipitous combination of styles made the original east siders appear to have far more power—and perhaps appear to be more of a threat to the council majority—than their two votes might warrant.

Since Des Moines adopted districts in 1967, we had the opportunity to observe at least the outlines of the maturation of the district system in that city. The stark east-versus-west battle lasted until the second election after the structural change when, in 1971, an east sider was elected to an at-large seat. This council member was even more outspoken—opponents would say outrageous—than "East Side 1," particularly on matters of ideology somewhat removed from the normal concerns of the Des Moines council. As shown in Table 6.12, this new councilman, labeled AL2, replaced ES1 in what had been the East Side bloc, while ES1 moved to a kind of "negotiation" or swing position. In fact, the minority bloc is more correctly described as a "conservative" bloc; ES1 remained a staunch advocate of benefits for his district, while AL2 opposed spending proposals even if east side projects were included.

Table 6.11. Percentage Agreement on Split Votes,
Des Moines, Term D2 (N = 94)

	AL1	AL2	West Side 1	West Side 2	East Side 1	East Side 2
AL1	X	81	78	80	42	21
AL2		X	68	62	41	21
WS1			X	78	38	17
WS2				X	36	16
ES1					X	63
ES2						X

Table 6.12. Percentage Agreement on Split Votes,
Des Moines, Term D3 ($N = 50$)

	AL1	West Side 1	West Side 2	East Side 1	East Side 2	AL2
AL1	X	93	94	65	20	17
WS1		X	93	65	12	19
WS2	"Negotiator"		X	62	22	22
ES1				X	47	40
ES2				Conservative Bloc	X	67
AL2						X

In more recent years, a strain of geographic/class conflict remains in Des Moines politics and among council members, but due in large part to the ability and interests of the "second generation" representatives from the east side, it is a somewhat muted conflict. These council members appear to be more concerned with district facilities and the problems of individual constituents than with ideology, and the council seems to be, at least on the surface, a much less fractious body than in the past.

Montgomery: Mayoral Clout

Although race was not the major issue in the change from commission to mayor-council government in Montgomery, most observers and council members describe that assembly as divided along racial lines. And, given a membership composed of five whites and four blacks in a city where blacks had not won election to the old legislature, such a division might almost be assumed. However, this was not the case in Montgomery's first district council, for voting configurations were linked more clearly to the actions of a strong mayor than to race.

During the second year of mayor-council government, Mayor Robinson resigned over police handling of an incident in which an officer shot a fleeing robbery suspect. (Robinson felt betrayed in his support for the findings of a police investigation which he later concluded to be a coverup.) He was replaced by council chairman Emory Folmar. Since that time, Folmar has used both the formal powers of a strong mayor and an open strategy of rewarding council supporters with city facilities and services to maintain a council majority which includes black representatives. As indicated in Table 6.13, two blacks were rather firmly attached to the mayor's coalition during the D1 term. While there may have been some clearly racial votes cast by this council, they were not its dominant feature. There was and is, however, frequent public conflict

Table 6.13. Percentage Agreement on Split Votes,
Montgomery Term D1 (N = 153)

	Whites					Blacks			
	9	7	8	2	1	5	6	3	4
9	X	76	74	75	74	69	63	47	44
7		X	69	77	70	60	50	37	29
8			X	83	70	69	57	48	36
2		Mayor's Bloc		X	77	73	67	55	43
1					X	73	71	49	48
5						X	74	64	49
6							X	57	57
3						Blacks		X	58
4									X

and bitterness between the mayor and one of the black councilmen (District 3); in fact, turnover in the black membership has resulted in increased racial polarization in the D2 council. One of Folmar's black supporters (District 6) was defeated in the 1979 election by an ally of the mayor's chief antagonist, and these two are often part of a three or four-member anti-Folmar bloc on the current council. Others in that group include the new black representative in District 4 who replaced an eccentric woman who had frequently missed council meetings, and a white councilman who opposes the mayor's tactics of using public resources as political patronage.

Several factors suggest that an escalation of racial conflict on the Montgomery council is possible, or even probable, in future years. Only one black member currently supports the mayor with regularity; because of this, he might be politically vulnerable in his district. On the other hand, of course, most observers believe that because of the councilman's allegiance to the mayor, that district has received more benefits than other black areas. Still, due to turnover in membership, black council opposition to the mayor has accelerated as the new system has matured. Folmar used his office as a springboard to nomination as the 1982 Republican candidate for governor of Alabama. However, if his successor continues the style of leadership he has established, with whites apparently assured of winning five of the nine council seats, future coalition formation will depend largely on the styles and goals of representatives from the black districts. It would not be surprising to find coalition formation on the Montgomery council become quite similar to that found in Richmond. Such a result would, of course, be a direct conse-quence of district elections.

Fort Worth: Factions, Texas Style

Roll call votes cast on contested issues in Fort Worth's at-large councils did not fall into any identifiable pattern; agreement seemed almost random in both the D-2 and D-1 councils. In the D-2 term, only three of a possible thirty-six council pairs voted together over 60 percent of the time; in D-1, only one council pair reached an agreement level of 60 percent.

After districts, however, coalition formation become an important factor in council decision-making. The Fort Worth factions are frequently described by two kinds of divisions: Attachments or opposition to downtown business interests, including developers, and ideological disagreements between conservatives and liberals. As might be expected, the more conservative members usually fall into the prodowntown camp, while liberals become part of the antibusiness faction. However, there is not a one-to-one relationship between these two areas of conflict. In fact, during the D1 term, the "downtown/conservative" bloc was comprised of white representatives from relatively affluent areas (Districts 3 and 7) and the council's two blacks, elected from poor majority-black districts. The opposing coalition, linked during the D1 term to the incumbent mayor, included three whites—a conservative, a moderate liberal, and a liberal—and the council's only Mexican-American.

While the "downtown" bloc appears to be the stronger of the two, both are evident in all split votes as well as in votes on specific policy issues. In Table 6.14 we show the coalition parameters for votes on plan-ning and zoning, issues which were central to bloc formation. The blocs were equally evident on questions of structure and process (see Table 6.15), public safety and social minimum, even though there were not many split votes—sixteen and eleven respectively—on the latter issues.

Three changes in council incumbency between D1 and D2 had a con-siderable impact upon the coalitions. A conservative replaced the liberal member, a new representative was elected to replace a former member of the "liberal" bloc who was elected mayor, and a new black represen-tative was elected in the Fifth District. As shown in Table 6.16, both white freshmen moved firmly into the "downtown" coalition. Coin-cidentally, the blacks—the veteran as well as the newcomer—became less firmly attached to that group. Finally, the remaining "liberal" pair has a rather low level of agreement. By comparing split votes on planning and zoning with those on structure and process—the most conflictual issues

Table 6.14. Percentage Agreement on Split Votes on Planning and Zoning, Fort Worth, D1 Term (N = 90)

| | Districts | | | | | | | |
	3	7	5	8	9	6	4	2
3	X	81	70	64	37	54	61	49
7	Downtown Bloc	X	61	71	52	53	46	42
5			X	66	62	68	62	57
8			Black Pair	X	61	48	55	53
9					X	73	67	52
6				"Liberal" Bloc		X	67	53
4							X	55
2								X

during the D1 term—we find that with the exception of one pairing on the former issue, the four whites in the "downtown" coalition had very high agreement levels (See Tables 6.17 and 6.18). While the evidence is very mixed, the black members seemed to move away from their former bloc, but did not move firmly toward the liberal pair.

Charlotte and Raleigh: "Modernization" and Opposition to Development

District efforts in the two Carolina cities were motivated in great part

Table 6.15. Percentage Agreement on Split Votes on Structure/Process, Fort Worth, D1 Term (N = 52)

| | Districts | | | | | | | |
	3	7	5	8	9	6	4	2
3	X	90	76	69	34	39	35	29
7		X	67	60	36	55	34	33
5	Downtown Bloc		X	70	39	27	27	35
	Black Pair							
8				X	41	38	36	30
9					X	49	92	70
6				"Liberal" Bloc		X	67	51
4							X	66
2								X

Table 6.16. Percentage Agreement on Split Votes,
Fort Worth, D2 Term (N = 179)

	Districts							
	3	7	9*	6*	8	5*	4	2
3	X	76	81	76	54	56	45	45
7		X	85	76	55	57	41	41
9	Downtown Bloc		X	78	54	60	44	40
6				X	58	67	51	48
8			Black Pair		X	69	38	53
5						X	54	72
4					"Liberal" Pair		X	52
2								X

*Nonincumbents.

by neighborhood activists who resented the dominant role of developers and downtown interests in their cities' decision-making processes. However, council coalitions which emerged in postdistrict Charlotte and Raleigh do not consistently reflect a neighborhood/downtown dichotomy.

As we have previously noted, several young professional men and

Table 6.17. Percentage Agreement, Split Votes on Planning
Zoning, Fort Worth, Term D2 (N = 68)

	Districts							
	3	7	9*	6*	8	5*	4	2
3	X	84	94	61	58	58	30	48
7		X	84	83	78	55	35	55
9	Downtown Bloc		X	92	58	58	30	48
6				X	65	64	40	52
8			Black Pair		X	57	29	61
5						X	49	55
4							X	52
2						"Liberal" Pair		X

*Nonincumbents.

Table 6.18. Percentage Agreement, Split Votes on Process/Structure, Fort Worth, Term D2 (N = 18)

	3	7	9*	6*	8	5*	4	2
3	X	85	92	69	64	36	9	27
7		X	89	72	61	59	22	47
9	Downtown Bloc		X	83	50	25	22	53
6				X	89	73	17	60
8					X	67	39	53
					Black Pair			
5						X	41	65
4					"Liberal" Pair		X	35
2								X

*Nonincumbents.

women joined the Charlotte council for its D–1 term. As seen in Table 6.19, four of the five newer members of this at-large council tended to vote together when there was disagreement, as did three veteran members. In the first district council, as shown in Table 6.20, the split-vote coalitions became more ideological and class oriented. The bloc found in the top left portion of Table 6.20 consisted of the two most conservative at-large members and representatives from the two most affluent districts (Districts 6 and 7). The other major coalition, the bloc found in the bottom right portion of the

Table 6.19. Percentage Agreement on Split Votes, Charlotte, Term (N = 259)

	Newer Members			"Old Guard" Members			
	A	B	C	D	E	F	G
A		44	39	41	47	42	44
B			63	70	67	53	60
C				81	67	55	58
D					73	61	66
E						76	76
F							79
G							

Table 6.20. Percentage Agreement on Split Votes, Charlotte, Term D1 (N = 380)

	AL1*	AL2	7	6	AL4	5	4	1	3	2	AL3
AL1	X	75	66	73	73	67	68	56	69	65	72
AL2	"Affluent X Conservative"	65	73	70	62	61	53	66	62	64	
7	Bloc		X	69	67	69	63	64	63	59	58
6				X	67	64	58	50	65	56	59
AL4					X	80	81	77	78	73	78
5						X	80	72	68	66	68
4	"Less Affluent/Liberal" Bloc						X	79	75	75	76
1								X	69	69	72
3									X	80	83
2						Black Bloc				X	80
AL3											78

*AL1 is a moderate. AL2 is an "old guard" businessman/politician. AL3 and AL4 are liberals, AL3 is black. The five districts with white representatives are ordered left to right by affluence. Districts 3 and 2 are represented by blacks.

table, included a black at-large representative, a white "liberal" at-large member, two black district members (Districts 3 and 2) and representatives from a racially mixed district (District 1) and from two middle class areas (Districts 5 and 4). Within this second coalition is the black voting bloc; these three councilmen voted together on at least 80 percent of the contested issues. Thus while overall conflict did not increase with the introduction of districts, it took on a new form. And the majority voting bloc in Charlotte's first district council did reflect the unique pattern by which the district referendum passed in that city, an observable if not conscious alliance between black and less affluent white voters.

These council coalitions were not very long-lived, however. As seen in Table 6.21, there were no strong, consistent voting configurations in the D2 term. While we have identified two rather loose blocs—first, the four at-large members with representatives of the two wealthiest areas, and second, representatives from the three poorest districts—these are very tenuous groupings. And when we look at votes cast on disputed questions in the two issue areas which engendered the greatest proportions of split votes, we find two different voting patterns. On questions of zoning and planning, three of the at-large members frequently voted with the representative from the city's wealthiest district (see Table 6.22). An even stronger bloc includes represen-

Table 6.21. **Percentage Agreement on Split Votes,**
Charlotte, Term D2 (N = 162)

	AL2*	AL3*	7	6	AL1	AL4	5	4	1	3	2
AL2	X	80	58	76	76	74	50	70	58	50	69
AL3		X	61	75	72	70	55	61	53	48	66
7			X	48	51	67	74	63	51	51	59
6	"At-Large" Affluent Bloc			X	74	71	42	63	48	46	69
AL1					X	75	52	67	50	56	68
AL4						X	69	87	70	75	71
5							X	83	58	60	49
4								X	80	71	68
1									X	57	60
3										X	60
2							Least Affluent Bloc				X

*Nonincumbent

Table 6.22. **Percentage Agreement, Split Votes on Zoning/**
Planning, Charlotte, D2 (N = 31)

	AL2	AL3	AL4	7	6	AL1	5	4	1	3	2
AL2	X	84	84	68	60	56	60	70	72	47	47
AL3		X	75	60	68	58	62	52	58	58	57
AL4			X	70	68	68	70	74	75	70	76
7				X	39	50	70	83	76	61	59
		"Affluents"									
6					X	54	33	38	32	30	65
AL1						X	45	50	48	54	62
5							X	88	82	61	61
4			"Neighborhoods"					X	91	65	61
1									X	67	59
3							Blacks			X	59
2											X

tatives from two middle-class suburban-type districts and the district with many racially diverse and "gentrifying" neighborhoods. Neither the two representatives from the wealthiest areas (Districts 7 and 6) nor the two from majority black areas (Districts 3 and 2) formed consistent voting pairs on planning and zoning issues.

Bloc patterns were far different on social minimum issues, as indicated by Table 6.23. Rather uniquely for the Charlotte council, votes appear to be cast in terms of race: The nine whites voted together quite consistently, and the two blacks voted together over 90 percent of the time.

At least some of the difference in coalition formation between the D1 and the D2 councils can be explained by a single idiosyncratic factor, a new representative filling one of the at-large seats. The only black at-large member generally acknowledged as the leader of the black council contingent had resigned his seat to run for mayor. He was replaced by a white member strongly supported in the upper-income areas. Overall, as the centrality of the development issue has receded somewhat, across-the-board coalitions in Charlotte have been replaced by a complex pattern of issue-specific alliances and individual friendships and antagonisms.

Raleigh's D-2 period must be interpreted in light of the small proportion of split votes in that period on any issue. Furthermore, although

Table 6.23. Percentage Agreement, Split Votes on Social Minimum Issues, Charlotte, D2 Term (N = 12)

	Whites								Blacks		
	AL1	AL2	AL3	AL4	7	6	5	4	1	3	2
AL1	X	75	75	90	75	75	92	90	90	36	32
AL2		X	83	100	83	83	83	83	80	18	17
AL3			X	90	83	100	83	83	80	27	17
AL4				X	90	90	100	100	100	33	40
7		Whites			X	83	83	83	80	27	17
6						X	83	83	80	25	17
5							X	100	100	36	33
4								X	100	36	33
1									X	33	40
3							Blacks—			X	91
2											X

there was some variation in agreement among pairs of members, there are no sharp splits (See Table 6.24). Everyone was tied into the group by a rate of over seventy-percent agreement with at least one other member. The most tightly knit group was that led by Mayor Seby Jones, which included the only black member. This consensus continued into the D-1 period, disturbed only by the entry on council of an ascerbic political activist in the populist mold (See Table 6.25). As happened in the last at-large council in Richmond, a lone dissenter caused overall rates of dissent to rise, but made the other six members appear even more consensual and certainly had little effect on council decisions.

Districts brought a complete change in council composition. The new system included direct election of the mayor, who would no longer have a council seat. The black council member was elected Raleigh's first mayor under this system.

The first district council began with no ties to past alliances. Given that most members had been elected on what was presumed to be a tide of antidevelopment sentiment, they seemed to follow a single mandate. Even the at-large and upper-income district representatives were moderates on the central questions of planning and growth. There was certainly no distinction between an at-large and upper-income group, on one hand, and lower-income and black members on the other (See Table 6.26). The most one can identify are dyads of personal friendship or antipathy, and the latter should not be exaggerated in an overall context of consensus.

The overall level of disagreement rose substantially in the D2 term, and there is movement toward two admittedly porous coalitions. The rough parity of forces can be seen in Table 6.27, a matrix based on all split votes cast during D2. The table shows "development" and "neighborhood" coalitions, but they are so tenuous that the black

Table 6.24. **Percentage Agreement on Split Votes, Raleigh, Term (N = 96)**

	1	2	3	4	5	6	7
1	X	75	76	75	71	71	44
2		X	76	78	57	69	59
3			X	73	64	63	51
4				X	46	74	63
5					X	43	37
6						X	71
7							X

Table 6.25. Percentage Agreement on Split Votes,
All Issues, Raleigh D-1 Term (N = 172)

	1	2	3	4	5	6 (Black)	7 (Lone Dissenter)
1	X	70	76	64	71	63	26
2		X	79	69	79	61	24
3			X	70	76	63	28
4				X	72	68	44
5					X	80	42
6						X	39
7							X

representative and one of the at-large members fall into both blocs. No firmer attachments to voting groups are found when split votes are examined by issue area. Blocs are simply not the rule on the Raleigh council, and voting in that body was almost as fragmented after districts were added as before the change in composition.

Districts and Coalition Formation

In most cases, districts have had some effect on the formation of voting blocs on our councils. For the period immediately following the adoption of districts, our hypothesis appears to hold. When previously underrepresented groups sent members to council for the first time, the extent of bloc voting by those members was related to cohesiveness among that group as well as its involvement in the district effort. Richmond's blacks and Des Moines's east siders were organized politically, and actively sought a larger voice in their local governments. Further, when blacks are elected to a substantial number of council seats, the

Table 6.26. Percentage Agreement on Split Votes,
Raleigh D-1 Term (N = 142)

	AL2	E	A	C	AL1	D	B
AL2	X	70	55	65	70	44	80
E		X	50	70	65	41	63
A			X	47	64	50	51
C				X	59	36	58
AL1					X	67	76
D						X	54
B							X

Table 6.27. **Percentage Agreement on Split Votes,**
Raleigh, D2 Term (*N* = 326)

	Upper Income				Black	Middle Income	
	AL1	E	A	AL2	C	B	D
AL1	X	66	54	52	49	51	52
E		X	67	75	64	73	62
A			X	61	57	58	59
AL2				X	73	86	60
C					X	76	75
B						X	76
D							X

possibility of bloc voting is always present, although this is probably less likely on the local level than in larger legislative bodies. It is difficult to predict what kind of impact districts will have on coalition voting in general and in the long run. We have seen that turnover in the membership of several of our councils had extensive consequences for coalition maintenance. In fact, with a very few exceptions, it is extremely difficult to explain voting patterns in terms of district characteristics. *Who* a district elects is a more important variable than whom and what he may represent.

CONTENT OF COUNCIL AGENDAS

It was hypothesized that district representatives would devote more time to routine decision-making concerning the placement of water and sewer systems, street maintenance, and so on. In other words, we predicted that the bureaucratic routinization of such decisions would be upset by the "politics" introduced by district representatives.

Findings from the eight cities for which we gathered roll call and interaction data give little support to that prediction. As Tables 6.28 and 6.29 show, only the Richmond council increased the attention given to routine matters after the change to districts. Votes on such topics as street repairs, traffic patterns and waste disposal rose from 17 percent of the Richmond council's roll calls in D–2 and 20 percent in D–1 to 31 percent in D1. This change may only be temporary, however, as the proportion of routine votes falls to 25 percent during D2 term.

Council interactions in both Charlotte and Raleigh show a dramatic reversal of the hypothesis (See Table 6.29). In Charlotte, the proportion of interactions devoted to routine matters was already decreasing in the predistrict councils, from 45 to 30 percent, and it fell to just 17 percent of

Table 6.28. **Proportion of Votes on Routine Services**

Term	Charlotte	Des Moines	Fort Worth	Memphis	Montgomery	Raleigh	Richmond
D-2	50.5 (1114)	34.7 (60)	85.4 (3279)	38.3 (51/133)	—	29.9 (1025)	17.5 (67)
D-1	28.0 (492)	39.5 (81)	84.3 (4021)	19.7 (37/188)	23.5 (495)	29.5 (1092)	20.5 (81)
D1	20.0 (494)	31.7 (106)	83.3 (4924)	39.0 (56/154)	23.3 (304)	26.9 (1100)	31.0 (205)
D2	32.0 (328)	37.8 (125)	87.9 (6612)	32.0 (41/128)	—	27.7 (976)	25.0 (142)

Table 6.29. Proportion of Interactions on Routine Matters

Term	Charlotte	Raleigh	San Antonio
D–2	44.8	47.8	20.6
D–1	30.3	50.7	20.6
D1	17.0	18.6	15.3
D2	—	40.3	25.1

the total in the first council after the adoption of districts. In Raleigh, routine matters dropped from 50 to 28 percent before districts, then to 20 percent during the first term with district members. While the proportion increased to 32 percent in the second postdistrict council, we cannot say whether this is part of an upward trend or simply a temporary phenomenon.

The addition of district seats had almost no effect upon the proportion of votes cast on routine matters by the councils in Des Moines, Forth Worth, and Raleigh. Although the percentage of routine votes in Memphis increased from D–1 to D1, the proportion at D1 is almost identical to that at D–2. Our conclusion must be that the hypothesis is not supported. If there is greater involvement of district representatives in decisions concerning routine city services, such involvement must take place outside the council chambers.

Although there were no hypothetical expectations that agenda proportions of any of the other issue areas would change after adoption of districts, we did examine our data for such unexpected results. We found none, other than one-term changes which could easily be traced to unique events or situations in a given city at a given time. In fact, we are inclined to doubt whether council composition can affect formal agendas in any kind of systematic manner, that is, over time and across councils. Preparation of the agenda is often left entirely in the hands of the city manager, and sometimes in the hands of a strong mayor. Local and state laws may require councils in some cities to vote on thousands of minor questions, while other councils rarely deal with questions of the day-to-day operation of their cities. Idiosyncratic factors abound in local politics and government: Particularly fractious individuals will serve on council during certain terms, specific policy issues or community conflicts will dominate certain other terms. Disrict representation is much more likely to affect council levels of conflict and consensus than to influence the formal agendas of these local legislatures.

NOTES

1   Our intent was to record and analyze all votes in at least the two council terms just prior to districts and the first two terms under districts. In most cases, we achieved this objective. In several cities, however, the number of votes, limitations on researchers' time, and the method of recording and filing records compelled us to do some sampling: In Des Moines and Richmond, the sample is of all votes on one year of a two-year term. All votes are included for Charlotte, Fort Worth, Memphis, and Raleigh.

2   An interaction is defined as a single uninterrupted statement by any person whose remarks are recorded in the minutes. Interactions were sampled according to the following procedure: Coders obtained a total sample of 1,000 communications before districts and 1,000 after districts. These were drawn in clusters of ten contiguous communications—100 clusters of 10 messages each, spread throughout the three terms before districts, and again in the total time period since districts. The first cluster in each period was determined through a random number selection of one of the first ten pages of minutes, starting with the first whole communication on the first page selected. Thus, in Charlotte, 1,000 codings were obtained out of the two years after districts by coding 10 communications every thirty pages of minutes.

7

Policy Consequences of
The Change To Districts

I N EARLIER CHAPTERS, we cited the considerable literature which informed our discussion of the demand for and the representational consequences of district elections; indeed, further study of this topic would probably be redundant. The field of past research was far less crowded when we looked at the impact of electoral structure on the formal and informal processes of local legislatures. Finally, no prior work has been done on a question which is central to the evaluation of local electoral systems, the question of whether the adoption of district representation has any observable influence upon government actions. Despite this lack of systematic evidence, claims made by both advocates and opponents of districts are often based on an implicit assumption that changes in representation will automatically translate into changes in policies, programs and distribution of resources. We turn now to a consideration of that assumption.

The impact of districts on representational equity for geographically concentrated minorities has been conclusively demonstrated. Whether that improved representation results in additional or improved benefits from local government is the question we must now address.

One should be cautioned, in any search for policy consequences, to avoid the "fishing expedition." Guides to social science research and common sense both suggest that, if enough variables are examined, a certain proportion will be interrelated. We seek to avoid that pitfall by focusing our attention on those areas of policy in each city that motivated citizens to become district advocates. By comparing what these advocates expected from districts with what they see as their achievements after districts have been in place for several terms, we should be able to identify intended effects of the change rather clearly. Any adjustment in political structures will have unintended effects as well, and where these are clearly linked to structure, they will be noted.

We have chosen to avoid the pitfalls of focusing our attention on year-to-year changes in municipal budgets. Budgetary analysts have uncovered a wide range of problems in a straightforward examination of dollars received and expended. First, they point to the fallacy of assuming that an increase in dollars spent has a direct relationship to service performance and productivity.[1] In fact, many recent studies of municipal services have avoided any direct reference to budgetary allocations altogether, and have looked exclusively at measures of service provision; that is, at productivity or at disparities according to ethnicity or class.[2] Second, there is the complex problem of interpreting city budgets. They are usually organized on the basis of a series of special funds, especially when certain types of revenues are earmarked for particular uses; any given function may be accomplished with resources from several funds, and the nonaccountant is poorly prepared to do the necessary compilations. Many cities have adopted program budgets that facilitate analysis by function, but categories are defined differently from one city to another, and funds other than the general fund may not be organized according to the same program breakdown.

There is yet another enormous difficulty involved in working with municipal budgets, the problm of discovering the specific origins, contributions, use and consequences of state and federal funding, and of matching intergovernmental resources to the functional breakdown used for locally derived money. The necessary unraveling for a single city is a vast undertaking in itself.

Some of these problems are avoided by the functional breakdown by city in the *Census of Governments* published by the Bureau of the Census. These, however, are produced only at five-year intervals, except for the *City Government Finances* series which is published annually, but which provides separate data for only the fifty largest cities.[3]

A problem of particular concern to our research is that it may not be possible for council members to affect the budget to any sizeable degree. Since cities are subordinate units of state government, the range of discretion of local decision making is limited. Allowable forms and levels of revenue are strictly defined; many expenditures are required by law or result from past commitments. The range of options available to a council may not be wide enough to demonstrate even a stark change in policy preferences.

Finally, and most importantly, our major concern is with the *geographic* distribution of city resources. Budgets may tell us that X dollars were spent on parks and recreation, but they do not tell us if 80 percent of those dollars were spent in one small area of a city, or if they were spread evenly across the city's neighborhoods.

For all these reasons, we have determined that the most useful approach to policy consequences is to chart district advocate preferences, to compare them with advocates' and local administrators' perceptions of results, and then bring to bear the available performance data relevant to the policy areas thus identified as related to district representation.

ADVOCATE PREFERENCES AND PERCEPTIONS OF CHANGE

Not all efforts to modify council composition are related to either specific, or even vague, policy goals, beyond the often unspoken assumption that changes in representation will translate into changes in policy. For example, in Peoria, the desire to add at-large seats to an all-district council can be traced to serendipitous factors which produced a council whose meetings were frequently likened to zoos and circuses. No specific policy goals are mentioned by district advocates in Memphis, where goals were primarily defined in political or representational terms. A similar situation was found in Montgomery. Finally, in Richmond, minority activists did not have district representation in mind when they began their litigation over the annexation of white suburbs. The original "advocate" was Curtis Holt, Sr., a physically disabled black with little formal education who ran for the at-large council from his public housing address. He filed the federal suit against annexation when he was edged out in an election that he felt he would have won under the previous city boundaries. He did not then, nor did he later, advocate districts, although it was his action that led to the structural change. Other black leaders publicly questioned whether they might not control local government more effectively through an at-large system.

A second pattern of links between district efforts and policy goals is the statement of nonspecific goals. Although some district advocates in Sacramento had no expectations of policy changes, others mentioned goals such as "more liberal policies," "better services to all geographic areas," and being "more active in seeking federal funds." In Des

Moines, two nonallied groups wanted districts for different reasons. The League of Women Voters supported the district plan as a means of saving city manager government. The east siders, on the other hand, not only wanted a voice in city decisions, but were demanding more and better facilities and services for their part of the city.

Even in those cities where advocates can articulate more specific expectations, there is an overriding impression of general feelings about equity and fairness. The common thread in these statements is that an establishment was running local government and that districts would democratize government institutions. This, indeed, became a self-fulfilling prophecy for the sizable proportion of advocates who themselves went on into elective or appointive office.

However, specific policy goals were a third motivation for districts. One of the most visible manifestations of at-large unfairness was in the ethnic, racial, and geographic distribution of appointments. This motive for districts was commonly advanced in Charlotte, Raleigh, and Fort Worth as an end in itself. Sometimes, of course, such an interest in appointments can be directed at specific positions with specific policy goals. One of the principal leaders of the district campaign from the lower-income west side of Charlotte was specific in requesting that his area be represented on the Airport Advisory Board, because the airport and its noisy side effects were problems in his part of town. He wanted a position on the Housing Authority, because a disproportionate amount of public housing had been built in that area. And he wanted a position on the planning commission for a watchdog against developer and landowner proposals to "downzone" in west-side neighborhoods. This clarity of purpose in seeking appointments was rather unique, however, among those advocates we interviewed.

Only a minority of these district proponents sought specific policy objectives, and they were from the subset of cities in which the change was the result of neighborhood and minoity pressure against reluctant incumbents. Routine services and facilities stand out as the most visible policy category in which to perceive inequity. The Des Moines east siders were particularly concerned about street paving and improved sewer systems. Charlotte west siders were most frustrated by the lack of council response to demands for an ambulance and emergency medical station. Another Charlotte advocate had waged a long campaign to have physical barriers and traffic signs erected to discourage traffic from cutting through her neighborhood. Charlotte minority supporters of districts had a similar list of specifics: Water and sewer extensions, sidewalks, paving, and streetlights. Such amenities as street cleaning and lighting were also mentioned in Raleigh, although they were of secondary interest there.

Complaints about protective services of the type the literature would suggest as a prominent minority concern were voiced only in Dallas, where minority leaders were advocating the creation of a civilian police review board and more aggressive efforts at minority recruitment in the police and fire departments.

Zoning and planning were central issues, of course, in the Charlotte and Raleigh changes, and here the advocates were most concerned with preventing past decisions from recurring. At-large governments, it was felt, had selected plans for traffic access to the central city that invariable involved throughways dividing middle- and lower-income neighborhoods. Similarly, some claimed to find patterns of haphazard and "strip" commercial zoning only in the unrepresented areas. The distribution of planning and redevelopment support offered by the federal government was not, however, an issue of concern to advocates; for most of them this was a new and unfamiliar terrain the potential of which they could not have recognized.

In the development policy area, the only advocate interest involved the distribution of parks and recreational facilities. A Charlotte neighborhood leader pointed out that her district had never had a park, and that a district representative would surely work to correct that inequity.

An overall assessment of these specific demands is that they focus almost exclusively on the geographic distribution of facilities and services. Although goals of redistribution among priorities within budgets surfaced after districts in those cities where the change radically redistributed council seats, nowhere did the advocates claim such a purpose during the struggle for structural change.

General Impressions—The Achievement of Equity

We have hypothesized that advocates would feel that improvements had followed the adoption of districts. However, there is no consensus on the general effects of districts among those who worked for the new systems.

There are citizen advocates who feel their goals were, on the whole, accomplished, that they have gotten what they expected and wanted out of districts. There is another large group of advocates, however, who feel either deceived or disappointed that changes in distribution never occurred or were only temporary. Advocate reactions seem uniformly negative in Dallas. This is generally true in Fort Worth as well, although one Hispanic respondent thought that blacks had made gains but that Mexican-Americans had not, and there is a perception of success in that city's distribution of council appointments. In Raleigh, there is consensus among advocates that the "business" interests have recaptured the government, although some say the early experience with districts has sensitized and moderated the business and development leadership. (Interestingly, the Director of the Raleigh Merchants' Association is still pushing for a return to an at-large system; the perception of who controls the government is not uniform.) In Charlotte and Des Moines, on the other hand, those who expected greater distributional equity and fairer representation in a general sense feel that this was accomplished, and that, if access to government services and the facilities is not completely equal, it is greatly improved from the at-large period.

Interestingly enough, administrators who might have initially been apprehensive of district representation have generally complimentary impressions of the new system. Some administrators, particularly in Dallas, feel that no change has occurred because none was necessary. According to one official, Dallas has used "national standards" in allocating resources and locating facilities for many years. Several Dallas department heads shared the perception of a Fort Worth official that they must react to district representation by giving council members a "systemic overview" on distributional matters; locational criteria and models are used in this process that "blunt" the district emphasis. These administrators pride themselves on the fact that they do not gather or report service and facility distribution by district, as administrators in other cities have done. However, Fort Worth administrators reported that they are now more conscious of districts in planning the capital improvement budget. Administrators in a majority of cities readily admit that changes have taken place, especially in large-scale allocations that are unavoidably part of the political process such as the siting of major facilities like airports, landfills, and throughways. Finally, a few department heads suggest that not all services can be allocated according to master plans and objective criteria; those that must be provided to some degree according to demand have felt a shift in that demand in accordance with change in the geographical distribution of the council.

COUNCIL APPOINTMENTS

Council appointments may be either substantive or symbolic, depending upon the role of the appointees. In line with our policy hypotheses, we would expect changes in substantive appointments only where district elections result in a new council majority.

The most important personnel decision made by councils in cities with council-manager governments is selection of the manager. As we previously noted, an incumbent manager was the center of constant, bitter conflict in the Des Moines council. However, only in Richmond did a district council remove an incumbent city manager: In the only city where districts resulted in a black majority, our prediction is correct. Mayor Marsh found his priorities at odds with those of Manager William Leidinger, and marshalled his coalition to abruptly fire him. Leidinger was, in fact, replaced by a black administrator; as a result of the change to districts the new mayor was able to bring the city administration under his control and keep it there until his loss of control over the council in 1982.

The change to districts may have induced the voluntary resignation of several other managers with strong leadership styles. Raleigh's manager resigned shortly after the referendum vote in favor of districts. Dallas's George Schrader resigned after six years under districts, during which time he openly expressed disapproval of the new system.

In addition to appointing the manager, councils make a large number of appointments to municipal boards and commissions, and thus indirectly extend their authority to a much wider body of decisions. Many of these groups are only advisory, as is usually the case of planning commissions, but their recommendations are often difficult to overturn; in fact, more than one council member has relied on the weight of a commission recommendation to "tie his hands" on a controversial issue. Other boards exercise considerable administrative authority, as (where these are municipal functions) in the case of boards of education and library boards. We have chosen what we consider the most substantive boards and commissions in our cities.

One advantage of using appointments as a test of policy consequences is that we can apply the same measures of equity as used in looking at representation. Board and commission appointments can be examined as to changes in the geographical distribution of members (by district of residence), and in the proportion of minority appointments. Our unit of analysis in measuring the spread of board and commission appointments is the term of appointment, counted by the number of appointments made in each term of council. Thus, an individual appointed to five consecutive terms on a board would be counted five times, if each appointment was under a different council term. If, however, a person filled the remainder of an unexpired term, then was reappointed for a regular term in the same council period, the combined service is counted as a single term of appointment. Although incumbents are often likely to be reappointed even in opposition to new distributions of political influence on a council, this approach seems most accurate in reflecting changes in council appointment patterns. Our data are limited to boards and commissions in existence through most of the two pre- and two post-change councils adopted as our standard framework of analysis. In addition, information on past boards and commissions were not available in all cities.[5] The advisory bodies we have selected for analyses are listed in Table 7.1.

These data combine appointments to all the commissions examined in each city. Overall trends in the proportion of minority appointments are shown in Table 7.2. There is a steady increase, generally, in minority presence among appointees; but as in other findings, there is no particularly sharp break in the trend between the D-1 and D terms. The greatest average increase is in the difference between D1 and D2, with Charlotte and Raleigh the only cities where the proportion of minority appointments peaks in the D1 period. However, there is a *decline* in naming of minority members between D2 and D3 in every city but Richmond.

Some of these findings must be explained on a case-by-case basis. In Richmond, the D period was only one year long, as an election long delayed by court order was followed by a return to the predistrict schedule. There were only fifteen appointments in that period, which makes it hazardous to define a trend. It appears, however, that the black council majority did not decide to increase the black membership on municipal commissions until the D2 period. Thereafter, we see a dramatic increase to 50 percent in that term followed by a majority of black appointments in D3. By the second year of the district system, the Commissions on the City Code, Council Agencies, Energy, Housing, Human Relations, Labor Relations, Transportation, Legislation, and the Regional Planning District all had black majorities. In San Antonio, on the other hand, there was a higher predistrict allocation of appointments from minority (mostly Mexican-American) groups and a less dramatic shift in commission membership. For example, there was evidently a pattern of balancing appointments among blacks, Mexican Americans, and "Anglos" on the fire and police and the general civil service committees both before and after districts. Thus the overall shift in the ethnic breakdown of appointments was slight, and resulted less often in black and Mexican-American majorities.

In Memphis, Charlotte, Raleigh, and Fort Worth, there is an upswing in minority appointments over the D-1 and D1 period that could be related to the new councils. However, these changes seem to be part of more wide-ranging secular trends in those cities, and are in line with the

Table 7.1. Boards and Commissions Included in Analysis Council Appointments

	Utilities	Civil Service Personnel	Housing	Planning/Planning & Zoning	Parks/Park & Recreation	Transit	Education	Welfare	Zoning Appeals Adjustment/Tax Equalization	Library	Facilities (Auditorium)	Area Fund/Urban Renewal Business District	Airport/Aviation	Memorial Fund
Charlotte	×							×			×	×		
Des Moines		×		×	×				×		×	×		
Fort Worth			×	×	×							×		
Raleigh	×	×	×	×		×		×	×		×			
Richmond	×	×	×	×			×				×			
Sacramento		×	×	×			×		×					
San Antonio	×		×	×				×	×				×	
Memphis	×		×	×							×			

Note: Records of Board and Commission Appointments are not maintained or were unavailable from Dallas, Montgomery, and Peoria.

Table 7.2. Percentage Minority
Appointments to Municipal Boards and Commissions

	D.2	D.1	D1	D2
San Antonio	42	43	45	47
Richmond	33	35	30	50
Sacramento	7	17	14	32
Fort Worth	27	19	26	28
Raleigh	12	21	25	18.5
Charlotte	5	16	20	17
Memphis	0	4	13	19
Mean	18.0	22.1	23.3	21.9

Note: Des Moines is not included because of its extremely small minority population.

view that transition to districts is itself a part of a larger cluster of political trends. In other words, it is as likely that increased minority representation on boards and the change to districts both resulted from more basic sociopolitical changes as it is that one in some sense caused the other.

In examining the distribution of appointments by district residence rather than by race or ethnicity, we can determine whether a wider distribution of political power is one of the consequences of newly districted councils. Presumably the concentration of at-large council members in upper-income neighborhoods should have resulted in a similar concentration of board appointments. Table 7.3 presents index values for the geographic distribution of appointments; a city would have an index value of *1* if appointments were distributed equally among the districts. For predistrict terms, the area from which a district was eventually formed was used as the geographic indication of that district.

Upper-income districts in each city were overrepresented in the predistrict period, although appointments were most out of proportion in all predistrict terms in Richmond, Charlotte and Des Moines. These are the only cases in which the change to district coincides with a dispersion of appointments away from upper-income districts, and the link to districts was most immediately apparent in Des Moines. As in most cities, the Des Moines council approves mayoral appointments to city boards; since the east side had only two of seven votes on the new council, the east siders could not have controlled appointments.

On the other hand, it is unlikely that other council members would have engaged in lengthy conflict over this matter; the presence of the

Table 7.3. Representation of Upper-Income Districts on Boards and Commissions

	D.3	D.2	D.1	D1	D2	D3
Charlotte	77/29 = 2.66	74/29 = 2.55	58/29 = 2.00	56/29 = 1.93	48/29 = 1.66	—
Des Moines	—	58/25 = 2.32	61/25 = 2.45	45/25 = 1.81	39/25 = 1.56	33/25 = 1.33
Fort Worth	42/25 = 1.69	40/25 = 1.60	62/25 = 2.45	52.5/25 = 2.1	43/25 = 1.73	—
Raleigh	66/40 = 1.67	76/40 = 1.90	46/40 = 1.15	64/40 = 1.60	66/40 = 1.64	68/40 = 1.70
Richmond	48/11 = 4.36	47/11 = 4.27	32/11 = 2.91	21/11 = 1.91	21/11 = 1.91	13/11 = 1.18
Sacramento	33/25 = 1.33	36/25 = 1.45	42/25 = 1.66	31/25 = 1.24	32/25 = 1.27	29/25 = 1.17
San Antonio	27/20 = 1.36	36/20 = 1.81	34/20 = 1.70	34/20 = 1.70	31/20 = 1.54	26/20 = 1.32

Numerator: percentage of appointees from upper-income districts.

Denominator: percentage of districts that are upper income.

If appointments were evenly spread among districts, the resulting index would equal 1.0.

outspoken east siders would probably have led to more appointments from their area regardless of original appointment lists. However, the new mayor, one of few business leaders to support districts, was intent on balancing the membership on boards and commissions, and his appointments of an increased proportion of east siders reflected that goal.

Our expectations concerning commission appointments are supported in the one black-majority city, Richmond. Similarly, they are supported by the absence of any sharp shift in control of advisory bodies in the other cities. Districts or mixed systems do not generally result in radically different appointment patterns.

It may be, however, that the nature of some appointments will change in other ways relevant to the intentions of district proponents. In an earlier chapter, we remarked on the "professionalization" of southern politics—in the sense that businessmen were being replaced as council members by those in professional occupations. While appointments to the planning commissions in four of the southern cities (Charlotte, Fort Worth, Raleigh, and Richmond) showed only a 14.5 percent increase in the proportion of minority appointments, the percentage of professionals among appointees increased by 33 percent; as a result, professionals have constituted the majority of planning commission appointments under districts in all four cities. A detailed occupational breakdown shows a reduction in the number of appointees from real estate and development backgrounds, a pattern of appointment which neighborhood activists supporting districts had regularly attacked as a form of self-regulation without protection of existing neighborhoods.

In sum, while changes in the background of board and commission appointees has been found in most of the cities on which we have appointment data, they are too gradual to suggest a link with district representation.

SPECIFIC EXPECTATIONS FROM DISTRICT REPRESENTATION

Turning to the specific goals of district advocates beyond the distribution of appointments, we hypothesize that substantive changes will result only where previously underrepresented groups gain a majority or near majority of the council.

First, advocates of improvement in routine services have in almost every case reported a considerable degree of success. Causal inferences by these political actors, of course, cannot be accepted at face value, both because perception may not always agree with reality, and because when it does, we may be observing changes that would have taken place with or without districts. Ultimately, however, the important political fact may not be whether change has taken place, but whether it has been perceived to take place.

There are still areas of east Des Moines with dusty, unpaved streets, but the number of such streets has been greatly reduced since the adoption of districts. However, we must be extremely careful not to assume a direct causal relationship between districts and paving.

Decisions about street paving in Des Moines are ultimately the council's responsibility. Each year, the city manager presents, for council approval, a list of streets selected for paving by his staff. Homeowners living on the streets are assessed for the improvements. However, if 60 percent of those who would pay 75 percent of the cost of paving their block signed a petition *opposing* the paving, the council has to unanimously agree that such a block be paved or it is removed from the list. For several years after the adoption of districts, the manager included many east side streets in his paving program, only to have them removed, after opposing petitions were presented, due to "no" votes by one or both of the east-side members. These "no" votes often reflected the immediate wishes of district homeowners to avoid an assessment, but they were votes *against* paving. The east siders' goal was to get the city to subsidize the assessments of their low-income constitutents.

It is in 1970 that we begin to find a different pattern of outcomes. First, the council gave the Southeast Area Planning Council a grant of $16,000 in response to resident protests that their area had been omitted from the Des Moines Model Cities program. Also, the principal street in the area commonly referred to as Southeast Bottoms was included in that year's paving program at no cost to neighborhood residents.

Most paving projects not requiring assessments were made possible by the increased availability of Model Cities funds after Des Moines was made a Community Development "Planned Variation" city in 1971. The initial Model Cities program was expanded to six areas, three on the east side, called Prime Service Areas. In a number of instances, PSA funds were used to subsidize the assessments accompanying improvements. A Southeast Bottoms sanitary sewer project was financed by a federal grant and local funds. In 1972, the council approved a project that virtually guaranteed free sewer hook-ups, sidewalks and street paving throughout the six PSAs; regardless of income or property ownership, residents of these areas would not be assessed for such facilities and improvements. This program was developed by residents of the PSAs, and approved by a 4-2 council vote; the majority included the two east side district members, the east-side at-large representative, and one of the west side district members.

We do not, in fact *cannot*, know if these and other similar decisions would have been made without district representation. Besides the improvements in streets and sewers, the years since districts have brought a variety of changes on the east side of the Des Moines River: These include an industrial/commercial development in the Bottoms—an impossibility before the new sewer systems—a new library, a new fire station, increased and improved ambulance service, and improvements in snow removal through the designation of snow routes. Des Moines's perceptive city manager says that these improvements would have been made regardless of districts "because they were needed." On the other hand, the most-skilled east-side representative credits much of the improvement to the opportunities provided by districts to voice his demands in a formal arena and to negotiate as a representative of roughly one-quarter of the city's population. In a very complex way, both views are probably correct.

Charlotte westsiders won their ambulance station, and, although they have continued to press for a dispersion of the city's medical facilities without additional success, they do perceive a more sympathetic hearing. Charlotte now has a policy of preventing traffic from cutting through neighborhoods, although causality is muddled here by the fact that the policy was adopted by the outgoing at-large council. District advocates will argue in such as case, of course, that the pressure for a district system forced the at-large body to be more responsive. Most advocates in Charlotte and Raleigh perceive greater fairness in decisions on water and sewer extensions, paving, and similar services, although they also sense that they have never been completely compensated for past inequities. Administrators respond that in cases where entire sections of a city were developed without such amenities, such compensation can only be gradual.

In the area of protective policy, advocates in just one city related their preferences to districts. Minority council members in Dallas led an unsuccessful attempt to create a civilian police-review board. They also pushed for greater efforts at affirmative action in the police and fire departments; assessments of their success in influencing Dallas's commitment to minority hiring vary widely.

Changes in city policies on zoning and planning might be reflected both in the change in backgrounds of council members, and in new appointments to the commissions that make specific recommendations in this area. It is quite clear that undesirable facilities can no longer be placed with impunity in middle- and lower-income areas of Charlotte and

Raleigh. This has become a major problem for Charlotte's current council, which has been unable to find an acceptable location for a critically needed new landfill. Zoning decisions are perceived by neighborhood interests in both cities to be more evenly applied, although they feel a need to pay constant attention to the activities of decision making bodies in this area.

The dispersion of parks and recreational facilities is, of course, a difficult and costly activity. The Charlotte neighborhood leader who singled this out as a special need seemed satisfied, however, that three parks are now in the planning stages for her district, even though none have been built.

It would appear that the administration of services over the long run has not been greatly affected by representational change, especially where bureaucrats had previously developed what they consider to be rational criteria of delivery. On the other hand, when the location of facilities requires a political decision, districts have been an important factor in bringing their advocates a considerable degree of success—or at least what those advocates *believe* to be a considerable degree of success.

Our null hypothesis that no substantive benefits would result from districts unless new council majorities were created cannot be supported by these findings. Neither, however, can we point to dramatic changes in the distribution of policy benefits over time, policy areas and cities. A vocal, determined minority of district representatives—or perhaps even a single, politically skilled district council member—can affect decisions concerning geographic distribution of goods and services. However, because the geographic variable looms so large in that type of decision, the overall impact of districts is probably overestimated by both district advocates and district representatives.

NOTES

1   See the discussion of this literature in Merget (1979: 176–178).

2   See Levy, Meltsner and Wildavsky (1974); Merget (1979: 178) refers also to Lucy and Mladenka (1978) as "an exciting study . . . building on this tradition."

3   The relevant census sources are: U.S. Department of Commerce, Bureau of the Census, *Census of Governments* (recently published in 1962, 1967, 1972, and 1977), and *City Government Finances* (published annually by fiscal year).

4   As in the case of our interviews with council members and city officials, we attempted to survey the complete universe of leading district representation advocates and opponents in each city. Obviously, this is a less clearly defined group, and again, we were limited in our success in some cases by the passage of time and

the disappearance of participants. Nevertheless, through a reputational approach (newspaper scanning and information from other interviewees), we identified and successfully interviewed forty-three advocates and nine leading opponents of districts in the eleven cities under study. The interview schedules for advocates and opponents are in Appendix A.

5   As has been noted by Clark et al. (1981), there is no readily available body of data on urban politics and government. City officials, quite understandably, keep records for their purposes, which often do not require maintaining the kinds of information on past events needed for research purposes.

8

Structure and Representation

T HE QUESTION, "Will districts make a difference?" has motivated our investigation of politics and government in ten large American cities; what would be the consequences, we asked, when district elections were established in cities which had previously chosen council members by the at-large method? Since effects of structural change might be found in many areas of public life including citizen participation representation, legislative behavior, and policy formulation, we have not based our development of hypotheses on any single theoretical perspective, but have instead drawn on a variety of past works.

In addition, some predictions were based on arguments advanced by district advocates in legal briefs and referenda campaigns. Advocates universally expected increased representational equity for groups disadvantaged by at-large systems, generally expected "things to be better" after districts, but only rarely articulated specific changes they expected to accompany the adoption of districts. However, as Eulau, Wahlke, et al. have said:

> Behind every proposal for altering the method of selecting officials is some assumption, at least, about the effect of such changes on what decision-makers or decision-making institutions

149

do, and how they do it. Proposals for reform must assume or
show that the proposed change will bring it about, that *what*
representatives decide and *the way* they reach decisions is more
nearly in accord with expectations and demands of the
represented than has been the case under the system to be
reformed.

(1959: 743)

We have, we believe, interpreted advocate arguments to bring at least
some of the specificity suggested by those authors to our hypotheses concerning the impact of districts. Because neither theoretical nor political
arguments suggest that district elections will automatically result in the
creation of new majorities, we did not begin with expectations of immediate dramatic changes in the distribution of either power or policy
benefits.

WHERE DISTRICTS MADE A DIFFERENCE

There is no question that blacks have achieved greater equity in local
representation as a result of movements to districts; this is the most obvious impact of changing local electoral structure. Also, it is clear that
district candidates spend less money than their at-large counterparts in
campaigning.

  While we incorrectly predicted a direct link between district
representation and ombudsman or delegate role-orientations regardless
of constituency characteristics, we discovered a striking relationship between those approaches to representation and election from nonaffluent
areas. Moreover, this change in representational style which we call the
emergence of the "aggressive ombudsman" was also obvious when we
looked at constituent contacts with council members: It is only members
representing a city's poorest districts who report receiving relatively large
numbers of calls for assistance. Although there is no such major change
in formal council proceedings, new council coalitions generally appeared
immediately following the adoption of districts. However, the new blocs
were most evident where previously underrepresented groups were
cohesive and had been involved in the district efforts; further, we believe
that such constituency-linked coalitions may be short-term rather than
long-run effects of shifts to districts.

  Turning to interactions between council members and city administrators, we found that the latter tend to believe that district
representatives will interfere with administrative procedures; on the

other hand, we found little evidence that such interference actually occurs or that if it does, that it disrupts established bureaucratic delivery rules. Finally, while we cannot identify dramatic shifts in the overall distribution of goods and services in any of our cities following the adoption of districts, the new systems of representation appear to be important factors in decisions concerning the geographical location of new city facilities.

AND WHERE THEY DID NOT

District representation does not result in electoral success for lower-status candidates, and there is only a marginal increase in the number of such candidacies. We found no support for two portions of the conventional wisdom concerning local electoral structure: Districts do *not* affect either voter turnout or the impact of campaign spending on outcomes. Further, although a few of our cities are the exception, district representation does not generally result in increased levels of conflict during council proceedings, nor does it lead to the addition of new or divisive issues to council agendas. Likewise, there is little evidence that district members, regardless of representational orientation or frequency of constituency complaints, engage in ongoing conflict with city administrators over the delivery of services. Finally, we found no evidence of major changes in the distribution of policy benefits, other than in the location of new facilities, and, in fact, found no consensus even among those who worked to establish districts as to the overall policy consequences of the new electoral systems.

THE ADVANTAGES OF DISTRICTS: EQUITY AND OMBUDSMEN

Our aggregate study of southern cities as well as our case studies provide further verification of the claim that geographically concentrated minorities will win far more district than at-large council seats. District elections *do* give previously underrepresented groups "their voice at City Hall." In some instances, the minority movement into city government may be a symbolic end in itself. In a few cases, where a "minority" may actually be, or be close to, a population majority, district elections can put control of the city government in their hands. This occurred in two of our cities, San Antonio and Richmond. However, in the Texas city, that control was short lived, as a five-member Mexican-American majority in the first district council reverted to an "anglo" majority in the next term.

Further, we have little evidence suggesting that the Mexican-American majority took any actions—or could have taken any actions, given the fiscal constraints under which today's cities operate—that greatly affected any group of San Antonio citizens. Similarly, beyond the vast symbolic benefits of a black-controlled government, it is difficult to point to any noticeable changes in the lives of Richmond's black citizens after two terms of a black mayor and a black-majority council.

In most cases, increased representation has been seen to provide no more than the possibility of increased influence over policy; it can never promise policy change. What the presence of district representatives does provide in most cases is personalized attention to the problems of district constituents in lower- and middle-income areas. And, borrowing from Fenno (1978), the "home style" of representatives from low-income districts is that of the ombudsman regardless of whether their "city hall style" is that of vocal dissent, quiet negotiation, or follow-the-leader.

DISTRICTS AND DISTRIBUTION: PERCEPTIONS MATTER

Des Moines and Charlotte provide the greatest evidence of observable changes in resource distribution among the areas and groups in each city since the adoption of districts; however, as we have pointed out, it would be incorrect to link these events in a strictly causal manner. Yet many advocates and neutral observers in these and most of our other cities conclude that, in the words of a Memphis advocate, ". . . [for minorities] simply being on the council is a resource." While optimistic conclusions are not universal, and some advocates are particularly disappointed with the lack of substantive results, we found far more satisfaction than dissatisfaction with district representation. A perceptive Charlottean stated that "I can't tell you exactly what it's done, but I know that everyone likes it." "Everyone has somebody on council looking out for them," was the view of one Montgomery city administrator.

Once again, it seems, perceptions focus on representation. It is quite likely that objective decision rules would result in equitable distribution of facilities and services, although certainly not equality of resources, regardless of council composition; that is certainly the view of the professional city employees we interviewed. But because district elections bring a diverse group of representatives to the council table, it can easily appear that this diversity automatically results in a fair distribution of public goods and services. And, finally, that diversity may well serve as a safeguard against attempts to continually favor one racial or ethnic group, one business interest, or one side of town, when council decisions concern public benefits.

THE FUTURE OF DISTRICT REPRESENTATION

We doubt that the lack of a consistant relationship between district representation and policy benefits for previously underrepresented groups—the results found in most of our cities—will discourage district advocates in other urban areas. This does not seem to be the kind of information that is transmitted from city to city, even though some organizations, especially the NAACP Legal Defense Fund, have been involved in many district efforts. Further, the assumption that more representation somehow automatically translates into more benefits seems to be held so universally and so strongly by district advocates that evidence from other cities would probably not dampen their enthusiasm.

Thus, we expect southern cities to continue the recent pattern of adoptions of either all-district or mixed-council systems. Advocates assume that establishing districts is worth the effort, and recent actions at the federal level are encouraging to prodistrict movements. In June, 1982, Congress passed and President Reagan signed a twenty-five year extension of the Voting Rights Act. The language of the extension was written to make clear to the courts that the intent of Congress is to prohibit election practices which have discriminatory *effect*. This language reverses the Supreme Court's *Bolden v. Mobile* decision which interpreted the Voting Rights Act as requiring demonstration of discriminatory *intent* before legal redress could be sought. The earlier position of the Fifth Circuit justices has been reinstated, and a new round of legal challenges to at-large systems has begun in southern and southwestern cities with histories of low representational equity. On the other hand, it is unlikely that districts will be sought by referendum in the future, except where racial or ethnic equity is not an issue. Local officials generally see further resistance as futile under the present wording of the Voting Rights Act (*Washington Post*, April 25, 1983). Many of those currently in power will attempt to forestall legal action aimed at establishing all district councils by drawing up their own plans for mixed systems or, perhaps, for systems in which candidates are nominated from districts but then elected at-large.

In any event, it seems clear that the question of local representation will continue to be a central issue in the politics of southern and sunbelt cities for the foreseeable future. It is not so clear that the actions of newly established district and mixed councils will make a great deal of difference in the lives of people who live in those cities.

REFLECTIONS ON STRUCTURAL CHANGE

The rules that define selection procedures are not neutral. Whether we focus on the method of selecting chairmen of congressional committees, on the manner in which delegates to presidential nominating conventions are chosen, or on the way in which city council members are elected, we find that different selection processes result in different "winners"; depending upon the procedure employed, those selected will represent varying interests, views, constituencies, and personal ambitions. Yet the central question that must be asked of any structural change concerns control: Will the change in rules result in the creation of a new power center or a new majority? In more theoretical terms, we suggest that although changes in selection procedures may result in variable shifts in the distribution of power, unless such structural modifications lead to a shift in control over decision making, the major consequences will be symbolic and stylistic. Future research into changes in selection processes will be misguided if it looks only for substantive consequences; such inquiries must be constantly aware that unless control is affected—unless major shifts in power occur—symbolic satisfaction and stylistic modifications will be the primary, not simply the secondary, results of structural change.

Appendix A

The council member role

1. What is the most important thing you as a council member do/did? If answer (a) "work for whole city," or (b) "look out for constituents":
2. What about (a) or (b)—(the one not mentioned)?
3. (If person has been both AL and Dist Rep) Did representing a district change your opinion in any way? How?
4. What activity took more of your time?
5. (If has/had staff) Which used more resources?
6. What about the people you've served with—how do you think they view(d) their role? Are/were you all alike or are there some different views?
7. When you vote/voted, do/did you ever feel your constituents might not agree with your vote?
   A. If NO—Do you think this is because you naturally think like them, or because you try/tried to find out what they want?
   B. If YES—Does this happen very often? On what issues? Do you get calls about this?
8. How often do you hear from constituents who want you to help them with an individual problem—a street light, their garbage hasn't been picked up—that kind of thing?

(they will answer "a lot," "sometimes"—try to get some quantification, if possible).

9.   (If person served on AL and district: Has this changed with the new council?
10. What do you do when you get these complaints?
11. What do you think the people in your district are most interested in—how you vote, or things you do for the whole district, or things you do to help people with specific problems?

The council process

1.   Is/was there much negotiating on votes?
2.   If "some" or "yes": who initiates it? On what kinds of issues?
3.   Is/were there people who vote/voted together most of the time?
4.   If yes, who are/were they? Did they vote together on all issues?
5.   Are/were you friendly socially with any of the other council people?
6.   (Yes or No): Does this make any difference to how you get along on the council?
7.   Is/was there any personal conflict—or any bitterness on your council(s)?
8.   If yes, what about?
9.   Was/is there a leader—or leaders—on your council(s)?

The City Manager

1.   How would you describe the ideal relationship between a council and a manager?
2.   How close does/did your council(s) come to this?
3.   If negative to #2, "Why is/was that?"
4.   Do you think a manager has ever had too much influence in (your city)?
     (If yes: when was that? How did it happen?)
5.   Was a manager ever too weak?
     (If yes: when was that? how did it happen?)

The Service Departments

1.   Does/did the council work directly with the service departments—fire, police, recreation, public works—the people who provide the services, or does/did it go to them just through the manager?
2.   IF DIRECT: What kind of relationships did you have? Were some better than others?
3.   Do/did you have any individual dealings—outside the council meetings—with these people?
4.   IF YES: What were these? Were you satisfied?
5.   Do you ever feel that any department treats different parts of the city in different ways?
6.   IF YES: What is that? What do they do? (probe for evidence) Have you tried to do anything about this? What was that? What happened?

7. (If on both AL and new): Do you think any people on the city staff, including the manager, have a different attitude toward the new council? If yes, who, what?
8. (If mixed council): Do you think anybody on the staff has a different attitude toward the district members as toward the AL members? If yes, who, what?

INTERVIEW SCHEDULE: CITY OFFICIALS IN POSITION BEFORE AND AFTER DISTRICTS

1. What dealings do you have with the city council as a part of the government?
2. Do you have any dealings with members of the council individually?
   (If yes—What are these about?) Probe for "troublemakers" and "good guys" and why).
3. Did you have dealings with individual members of the at-large council? What were these about? (See above)
4. Has the change in council made any difference to your department?
   (IF YES—what differences?)
5. How do you decide where and when to provide your services (adapt this question so that it makes sense. For example, for police, you would ask something like "How do you decide where to assign foot and car patrols?" The object is to get DECISION RULES concerning distribution of their service.)
6. Has anyone in a political job—a council member or the mayor—ever questioned the way you decide to provide your services? (is the new council different from the old in this respect.)
7. Do you get many complaints from residents about your service?
   ("yes" answers unlikely)
8. Is there a routine procedure for receiving complaints? (Describe)
   (If there are suggestions of "crackpot" complaints, or unreasonable complaints, do these come from only some areas of the city?)

For highest-level officials at the time of the change: (Mayor, Manager, etc.)

1. What did you think would occur, politically and substantively, if the change took place?
2. Have politics and the distribution of policy benefits changed since the new electoral system was established? If so, in what ways?

INTERVIEW SCHEDULE: ADVOCATES OF DISTRICTS

1. Why did you want districts?
2. What did you think would happen if council members were elected by

districts:

A. in politics? Did this happen?

B. in policy? (i.e., in what the council decided to do?) Did this happen?

3. Has anything else happened which you think is due to districts?

IF BY LITIGATION:

1. Was the decision to take court action triggered by a single incident (e.g., defeat of a minority candidate or a specific council decision) or was it the result of gradually escalating dissatisfaction with the at-large system?
2. What groups and individuals encouraged or advised court action? Who discouraged it? Was the referendum method of change ever considered?
3. Were leaders of the black or Mexican-American community(ies) united in supporting the action?
4. How strong was the city's opposition to changing the form of elections? Who, particularly, was in opposition?
5. What was the cost of litigation to local groups? How were these funds raised?
6. Were there any nonminority groups supporting the plaintiff's case?

IF BY REFERENDUM:

1. How did the referendum come about? Was the decision to seek a change the result of a single incident or of a gradual escalating dissatisfaction?
2. What group(s) took the lead in designing the proposal and getting it on a ballot? What did they do?
3. How much did it cost to get the proposal on the ballot? How was the money raised?
4. Were leaders of black, Mexican-American, or other minority communities united in supporting the action?
5. Were any white groups or neighborhoods in favor of the change? If yes, what did they do to support it?
6. What were the major campaign activities? (Ask specifically about precinct activity and media use if these were not mentioned.)
7. Who "ran" the campaign? How much did it cost? How was the money raised?
8. Did any people or groups get active in politics because of this campaign? Are they still active?
9. Why do you think the proposal passed?

Change of subject to city services and facilities

What do you think about the way services are provided by the city today?

2. If unhappy with some area: Have there been improvements in _____ since the council change? Have district council members been able to do anything about _____?

If Yes: What have they done? (get specifics)

If No: Have they tried? If so, why have they failed?

(If they haven't tried: Could a different kind of council member do more?

(If not mentioned above): "Have there been any changes in _____ since you got district people on the council?"

3. What about facilities—things like parks, libraries, sidewalks - has anything changed since the change in your council?

4. Do you get the feeling that in general, the council has a lot of control over the way services are provided?

   If No: Could something be done to get this kind of control?

   If Yes: Has this happened since the change in council?

5. Concerning services they are unhappy with: Who do you think is to blame for this situation? The people in charge of _____ or the people who do the actual work?

6. Do you know whether or not people in your organization—or in your community generally—complaint about _____ to city officials?

   If No: Why Not?

   If Yes: Whom do they contact?

   If council member isn't mentioned, ask: Do they ever contact their council member? (If no: Why not?)

INTERVIEW SCHEDULE: OPPONENTS TO DISTRICTS

1. Why did you prefer an at-large system?

2. What did you think would happen if council members were elected by districts:

   A. in politics? Did this happen?

   B. in policy? (i.e., what the council decided to do?) Did this happen?

3. Has anything else happened which you think is due to districts?

4. Do you still oppose districts? Do you think there might be an effort to go back to an at-large council?

If By Referendum:

1. Did you think the proposal would pass? Why or why not?

   (If not answered above, Why did it pass?)

2. Let me ask a few questions about the opposition to districts:

   A. Did you do anything to oppose bringing it to a vote? If yes, what was that?

   B. How was your group organized? Who was involved? Was there a leader or leaders?

   C. What things did you do to oppose the plan—what were your "campaign activities?"

   D. Do you remember how much this campaign cost? If yes, how did you raise the money?

E. What was the hardest part of the campaign?

If By Litigation:

1. Did the plaintiffs have a strong legal case?
2. What was the city's (or other defendent's) strongest legal argument?

References

Alford, Robert and Eugene Lee. 1978. "Voting Turnout in American Cities," *American Political Science Review* 62 (September): 796–813.

Bachrach, Peter and Morton S. Baratz. 1962. "Two Faces of Power," *American Political Science Review* 56 (December): 947–52.

Bales, Robert F. 1950. *Interaction Process Analysis*. Reading, Mass.: Addison-Wesley.

———. 1970. *Personality and Interpersonal Behavior*. New York: Holt, Rinehart and Winston.

Banfield, Edward and James Q. Wilson. 1963. *City Politics*. Cambridge: Harvard University Press.

Barber, James D. 1966. *Power in Committees*. Chicago: Rand McNally.

Browning, Rufus P., Dale Rogers Marshall, and David H. Tabb. 1979. "Blacks and Hispanics in California City Politics: Changes in Representation," *Public Affairs Report* 20 (No. 3). Berkeley: Institute of Governmental Studies, University of California.

Campbell, David and Joe Feagin. 1975. "Black Politics in the South: A Descriptive Analysis," *Journal of Politics* 37 (February): 129–159.

Clark, Terry N. 1968. "Community Structure, Decision Making, Budget Expenditure and Urban Renewal in Fifty-One American Cities." *American Sociological Review* 33 (August): 576–593.

———. 1981. Editor, *Urban Policy Analysis*. Beverly Hills: Sage.

Claunch, Ronald G. and Leon C. Hallman. 1978. "Ward Elections In Texas Cities," *The Municipal Matrix* 10 (No. 1, March). Denton, Texas: North Texas State University Center for Community Services.

Cobb, Roger W. and Charles D. Elder. 1972. *Participation in American Politics: The Dynamics of Agenda Building*. Boston: Allyn and Bacon.

Cole, Leonard. 1974. "Electing Blacks to Municipal Office," *Urban Affairs Quarterly* 10 (September): 17-39.

Cotrell, Charles L. and Arnold Fleischmann. 1979. "The Change from At-Large to District Representation and Political Participation of Minority Groups in Forth Worth and San Antonio, Texas," Paper presentation at the Annual Meeting of the American Political Science Association, Washington, D.C., August 20-September 3.

―――, and R. Michael Stevens. 1978. "The 1975 Voting Rights Act and San Antonio, Texas: Toward A Federal Guarantee of a Republican Form of Local Government" *Publius* (Winter): 79-99.

Cuomo, Mario. 1974. *Forest Hills Diary*. New York: Vintage.

Curtis, Tom. 1978. "Who Runs Cowtown?" *Texas Monthly's Political Reader (First Edition)*: 240-243. Austin: Texas Monthly Press.

Dahl, Robert A. 1961. *Who Governs?* New Haven: Yale Univsity Press.

―――. 1963. *Modern Political Analysis*. Englewood Cliffs, N.J.: Prentice-Hall.

Edelman, Murray. 1964. *The Symbolic Uses of Politics*. Urbana: University of Illinois Press.

Engstrom, Richard L. and Michael D. McDonald. 1981. "The Election of Blacks to City Councils: Clarifying the Impact of Electoral Arrangements on the Seats/Population Relationship." *American Political Science Review* 75 (June): 344-354.

Eulau, Heinz and Kenneth Prewitt. 1973. *Labyrinths of Democracy: Adaptations, Linkages, Representation and Policies in Urban Politics*. Indianapolis: The Bobbs-Merrill Co.

―――, John C. Wahlke, William Buchanan and Leroy C. Ferguson. 1959. "The Role of the Representative: Some Empirical Observations on the Theory of Edmund Burke," *American Political Science Review* 53 (September): 742-756.

Fenno, Richard R., Jr. 1978. *Home Style: House Members in Their Districts*. Boston: Little, Brown.

Fiorina, Morris P. 1977. *Congress: Keystone of the Washington Establishment*. New Haven: Yale University Press.

Hadden, Jeffrey K., Louis H. Masotti and Victor Thiessen. 1968. "The Making of Negro Mayors, 1967," *Trans-action* 5 (Jan.-Feb.): 21-30.

Harrigan, John J. 1981. *Political Change in the Metropolis*, 2nd ed. Boston: Little, Brown.

Hays, Samuel P. 1964. "The Politics of Reform in Municipal Government in the Progressive Era," *Northwest Quarterly* 55 (October): 157-169.

Hopmann, Terrence. 1974. "Bargaining in Arms Control Negotiations: The Seabeds Denuclearization Treaty," *International Organization* 28 (No. 3): 313-343.

Jones, Bryan D., Saadia R. Greenberg, Clifford Kaufman, and Joseph Drew. 1978. "Service Delivery Rules and the Distribution of Local Government Services: Three Detroit Bureaucracies," *Journal of Politics* (May): 332–368.

Judd, Dennis. 1979. *The Politics of American Cities: Private Power and Public Policy*. Boston: Little, Brown.

Karnig, Albert, K. 1976. "Black Representation on City Councils," *Urban Affairs Quarterly* 12 (December): 223–242.

———, and Susan Welch. 1980. *Black Representation and Urban Policy*. Chicago: University of Chicago Press.

Latimer, Margaret. 1979. "Black Political Representation in Southern Cities," *Urban Affairs Quarterly* 15 (September): 65–86.

Levy, Frank S., Arnold J. Meltsner, and Aaron Wildavsky. 1974. *Urban Outcomes*. Berkeley: University of California Press.

Lineberry, Robert. 1977. *Equality and Urban Policy: The Distribution of Municipal Public Services*. Beverly Hills: Sage Publications.

———. 1978. "Reform, Representation and Policy," *Social Science Quarterly* 59 (June): 173–177.

——— and Edmund P. Fowler. 1967. "Reformism and Public Policies in American Cities," *American Political Science Review* 61 (September): 701–716.

———, and Ira Sharkansky, 1979. *Urban Politics and Public Policy*. New York: Harper and Row (2nd edition).

Lowi, Theodore J. 1964. At *The Pleasure of the Mayor*. New York: Free Press of Glencoe.

Lucy, William H., Dennis Gilbert, and Guthrie S. Birkhead. 1977. "Equality in Local Service Distribution," *Public Administration Review* 37: 687–697.

——— and Kenneth R. Mladenka. 1978. *Equity and Urban Service Distribution*. Study conducted at the University of Virginia under contract to The Urban Management Curriculum Development Project, The National Training and Development Service. Washington, D.C.

Martin, John Bartlow. 1974. "The Town That Reformed," in John A. Gardiner and David J. Olson, eds., *Theft of the City* (Bloomington: Indiana University Press): 118–128.

Matthews, Donald R. and James W. Prothro. 1966. *Negroes and the New Southern Politics*. New York: Harcourt, Brace and World.

Mayhew, David R. 1974. *Congress: The Electoral Connection*. New Haven: Yale University Press.

MacManus, Susan A. 1978. "City Council Election Procedures and Minority Representation: Are They Related?," *Social Science Quarterly* 59 (June): 153–161.

Meltsner, Arnold J. 1971 *The Politics of City Revenue*. Berkeley: The University of California Press.

Merget, Astrid E. 1979. "Equity in the Distribution of Municipal Services," in Herrington J. Bryce, ed., *Revitalizing Cities* (Lexington, Mass: Lexington Books): 161–191.

Mundt, Robert J. and Peggy Heilig. 1982. "District Representation: Demands and Effects in the Urban South," *Journal of Politics* 44 (November): 1035-1048.

———. 1983. "Changes in Representational Equity: Effects of Adopting Districts," *Social Science Quarterly* 64 (June): 393-397.

O'Rourke, Timothy G. 1979. "The Legal Status of Local At-Large Elections: Racial Discrimination and the Remedy of 'Affirmative Representation'." Paper presented at the Annual Meeting of the Southern Political Science Association, Gatlinburg, Tennessee, November 1-3.

Pilat, Oliver. 1968. *Lindsay's Campaign*. Boston: Beacon Press.

Pitkin, Hanna F. 1969. *Representation*. New York: Atherton Press.

Pressman, Jeffrey L. and Aaron Wildavsky. 1973. *Implementation*. Berkeley: University of California Press.

Rakove, Milton. 1975. *Don't Make No Waves, Don't Back No Losers*. Bloomington: Indiana University Press.

Rauh, Joseph, Jr. 1968. "Political Participation," *Civil Rights Digest* 1 (Summer): 9-10.

Reiss, Albert J., Jr. 1961. *Occupations and Social Status*. Glencoe, Illinois: Free Press.

Robinson, Theodore and Thomas R. Dye. 1978. "Reformism and Black Representation on City Councils," *Social Science Quarterly* 59 (June): 133-141.

Sanders, Haywood T. 1979. "Government Structure in American Cities," *The Municipal Yearbook* (Washington: International City Managers' Association): 97-143.

Schattschneider, E.E. 1960. *The Semi-Sovereign People*. New York: Holt, Rinehart and Winston.

Schiesl, Martin J. 1977. *The Politics of Efficiency: Municipal Administration and Reform in America, 1800-1920*. Berkeley: University of California Press.

Sloan, Lee and Robert M. French. 1971. "Black Rule in the Urban South?" *Trans-Action* 5 (November-December): 29-34.

Sloan, Leonard. 1969. "'Good Government' and the Politics of Race," *Social Problems* 17 (Fall): 161-164.

Taebel, Delbert. 1978. "Minority Representation on City Councils: The Impact of Structure on Blacks and Hispanics," *Social Science Quarterly* 59 (June): 142-152.

Tucker, David M. 1980. *Memphis Since Crump: Bossism, Blacks and Civic Reformers, 1948-1968*. Knoxville: University of Tennessee Press.

U.S. Commission on Civil Rights. 1975. *The Voting Rights Act Ten Years After*. Washington: U.S. Government Printing Office.

Wahlke, John C., Heinz Eulau, William Buchanan and Leroy C. Ferguson. 1959. *The Legislative System: Explorations in Legislative Behavior*. New York: Wiley.

Walcott, Charles and P. Terrence Hopmann. 1978. "Interaction Analysis and Bargaining Behavior," in Robert T. Golembiewski, ed. *The Small Group in Political Science* (Athens: University of Georgia Press): 251-262.

Wirt, Frederick M. 1974. *Power in the City*. Berkeley: University of California Press.

Wolfinger, Raymond E. 1974. *The Politics of Progress*. Englewood Cliffs: Prentice-Hall, Inc.

Author Index

Subject Index